KNACK
MAKE IT EASY

COACHING
YOUTH BASEBALL

In
Memory
of

Jeffrey B. Robinson
1960 - 2010

KNACK

COACHING
YOUTH BASEBALL

Tips on Building a Winning Team

KEVIN T. CZERWINSKI

Photographs by Beth Balbierz

KNACK
MAKE IT EASY

Guilford, Connecticut
An imprint of Globe Pequot Press

MAKE IT EASY

Copyright © 2010 by Morris Book Publishing, LLC

Knack is a registered trademark of Morris Book Publishing, LLC, and is used with express permission.

Editorial Director: Cynthia Hughes
Editor: Katie Benoit
Project Editor: Tracee Williams
Cover Design: Paul Beatrice, Bret Kerr
Interior Design: Paul Beatrice
Layout: Kevin Mak
Cover Photos by: Beth Balbierz
Interior Photos by: Beth Balbierz with the exception of those on page 44 © Linda Bucklin | Shutterstock
Diagrams by: Lori Enik

Library of Congress Cataloging-in-Publication Data
Czerwinski, Kevin T.
  Knack coaching youth baseball : tips on building a winning team /Kevin T. Czerwinski ; photographs by Beth Balbierz.
     p. cm.
  Includes index.
  ISBN 978-1-59921-863-2
  1. Baseball for children—Coaching. 2. Youth league baseball—Coaching. I. Title.
  GV880.4.C94 2010
  796.357'62--dc22
                    2009048393

The following manufacturers/names appearing in *Knack Coaching Youth Baseball* are trademarks:
Akadema® Pro, All-American Girls Professional Baseball League®, All-Star Game®, Babe Ruth League®, Challenger Division®, Chicago White Sox™, Diamondbacks™, Dodgers™, Easton™, Gold Glove®, Hall of Fame®, Lena Blackburne's Baseball Rubbing Mud®, Little League®, Major League Baseball®, Major Leagues®, Marlins™, Mets™, Mizuno™ Sporting Goods, NBA®, PONY™ League, Rawlings™, T-Ball USA™, Tigers™, Velcro®, White Sox™, Wiffle®, Wilson® Sporting Goods, World Baseball Association®, World Series®, and Yankees™

Printed in China

10 9 8 7 6 5 4 3 2 1

This book is dedicated to my dad, Thomas Czerwinski. He introduced me to the sport, taught me how to play baseball, and showed me just how great a game of catch with your dad can be. It's also dedicated to my son, Thomas Czerwinski, a kid my dad would have been very proud of. I'm thrilled to be the conduit between them, taking what I learned from my father and passing it on to my son. He's a great little ballplayer and a pleasure to coach. This book is also dedicated to my younger son, Braden, who I am hoping will someday allow me to teach him as I have taught Thomas. Finally, this book is dedicated to my wife, Wendy, who helped put it together and keep it together when it seemed like the whole thing was just going to fall apart. She was patient and understanding at every turn. Like just about everything else in my life, this project wouldn't be complete without her.

Author Acknowledgments

I'd like to thank Beth Balbierz, a friend and colleague for many years, for getting me involved in this project. Her thoughtfulness and counsel have been a blessing. She remains the best photographer I have ever worked with, but more importantly she remains a friend.

I'd also like to thank Maureen Graney for her faith in me while giving me the opportunity to expand my horizons. Joseph Gilligan and the folks at Akadema in Hawthorne, New Jersey, also deserve thanks for letting us use their factory, their employees, and their equipment for many of the photos in this book.

Thanks to Helene Collins and the rest of the Suffern (NY) T-shirt Marlins for their help with this book as well. They were a pleasure to work with and be around. Hopefully, I'll get to spend more time with them in the future.

Photographer Acknowledgments

First, I would like to thank my family (Rob, Samantha, Derek, Mom, Dad, and Amy). Without them and their support I couldn't have finished this book. To my son Derek, who was so patient and understanding when he was a part of so many photo shoots. You're my baseball buddy! To Kevin Czerwinski, it was a pleasure to have the opportunity to work with you again after so many years. Your writing and knowledge of the game of baseball made this a book fun to photograph. Wendy, thank you for all of your hard work helping Kevin and me complete this project. For Thomas and Braden, you were great models.

I would also like to thank Helene Collins and the players of the Marlins Little League Team in Suffern, New York. You did an awesome job during our shoot. Thank You!! to Joe and Lawrence Gilligan and all the guys at Akedema, Inc. in Hawthorne. A huge thank you to my players, parents, fellow coaches, umpires, and friends at the Franklin Township Little League. All of you were a tremendous help to me during the photography of this book. Finally, I would like to thank Maureen Graney for bringing me on to this project; and Katie Benoit and Tracee Williams for helping me complete it.

CONTENTS

INTRODUCTION

The thought of coaching baseball has always been in the back of my mind. I played the game competitively when I was younger but realized as I made my way through high school that sometimes desire and skill don't exactly run neck and neck. At some point the glove and bat become a source of recreation as dreams of them providing a source of income become just that—dreams. When I came to this realization, playing baseball took on an entirely different meaning for me. Accepting that I would not be playing third base in the Major Leagues was not a life-altering event. Sure, I would have loved to have been a professional athlete for twenty years, playing in the pros and enjoying the benefits that come along with it. My life, however, turned out just fine. And baseball has remained a big part of it.

The fact that I've been able to spend most of my professional career immersed in the game, covering it, writing about it, talking about it, analyzing it, and even teaching it has provided me with nearly as much joy as playing it would have. I say nearly because I imagine that nothing would be able to match putting on a uniform and playing every day. Coaching it, though, comes pretty close.

I worked for Major League Baseball for eight years, spending countless hours at spring training and in ballparks throughout the country. I've gotten to know scores of baseball players, watched endless hours of batting practice, infield drills, bullpen sessions, etc. The lessons I've learned watching the pros and the discussions I've had with them regarding playing the game and how to approach it have been of immeasurable import. They've also had a great deal of impact on the way I coach and teach the game to my children and their friends.

Being able to take something I learned while watching Seattle's minor league field coordinator go through drills with a group of young infielders one afternoon in San Bernardino and impart that knowledge to a group of youngsters is exciting for me. Watching him teach a group of nineteen- and twenty-year-olds how to turn a double play more efficiently altered the way I viewed turning a double play and as a result, I took what I saw and incorporated it in my own style of coaching.

I was also fortunate enough to spend several years with former Mets infield coach Matt Galante, discussing the game with him and watching as he helped turn David Wright into a Gold Glove third baseman. He did one drill in particular with Wright that stood out. He had Wright set up on his knees and proceeded to bounce countless ground balls off his chest and arms. It taught Wright how to react quicker and was something that I stored away for when it was time to teach my own kids about playing ball.

I have also spent far too many hours to mention watching players stretch and prepare for games. While it may seem boring, being able to see how the pros prepare and get their bodies in shape wasn't wasted on me. I've incorporated some of what I learned and what I saw, putting it in this book in the hope that it will prevent some youngsters from getting hurt when they play.

Always room for improvement

Your parents and your teachers have hopefully drilled into you that you are never too old to learn. Watching ballplayers grow, whether they are playing in the local Little League or at Yankee Stadium, has reinforced my belief that you really are never too old to learn. I continue to grow as a writer, a

teacher, and a coach, learning every day, not only from my colleagues but from the children I work with as well.

There is always room for improvement, as a coach, as a player, and as a person; this may be one of the biggest points that I'm trying to make in *Knack Coaching Youth Baseball*. You can always learn something different and become better as a result of that knowledge, regardless of your age or where the knowledge originates from.

The opportunity to coach is a special one. You have the chance to help mold young people in such a way that when they look back on their childhood experiences, you will be remembered fondly. I still remember the coach I had in Little League, a great, energetic guy who took a lot of time and put in a lot of effort to make us better players and better people. He taught me much about the game and about life. When I ran into him years later as an adult, he was the athletic director of a local high school and had also spent

time as an NBA scout. I took the time to thank him for what he did for me when I was twelve years old because he made a difference in my life.

He taught me at an early age that a person's skin color didn't matter, that a person's skill level didn't matter, and that how you conducted yourself off the field was much more important than anything you would ever do on the field. Oh, and I also thanked him for showing me how to charge a bunt and field it bare-handed in time to make the throw to first base. The point of all of this is to say that baseball has played a huge role in my life. For years I've made my living by being around the game. I don't get paid to coach, though, and I don't want to get paid to coach. My reward has been watching my son develop as a player, watching him learn how to take an outside pitch the other way, and getting excited that someday he wants to learn how to throw a slider.

My payment has come when I tell a youngster to choke up on the bat because he'll be able to control it better and then watching him line a ball over short instead of striking out because he is swinging for the fences.

For the love of coaching

So take this book and use it. Teach your children and their friends about the game. I don't profess to have all the answers about coaching or parenting. No one can make that claim and expect it to be believed. Far be it for me to be that presumptuous. Everyone has his own life experiences, in and out of the game. What you will read about in *Knack Coaching Youth Baseball* is a product of mine. I have a wealth of experience, having spent nearly twenty-five years as a sportswriter. I've worked in print, on the Internet, and on television, writing about and discussing baseball.

Through all that, the purest form of baseball I've come across has been at the youngest levels. Watching kids learn about the game and discover the joys of playing it provides as much fun as watching the multimillionaires do it on television or at the ballpark.

You do not have to be a star athlete to be a good coach. A simple understanding of the game, a great deal of patience, and the desire to help these kids and enrich their lives is all it takes. Remember that baseball is something that can bind generations. It is something that a seventy-five-year-old grandfather can discuss with his fifty-year-old son and his twenty-year-old grandson and each of them can have the same level of passion about the topic at hand.

Baseball is fun, it is exciting, and every day something new and different can happen on the field, something that neither you nor your players have ever experienced before. Embrace the opportunity to coach and enjoy the time you have with the kids. It is something you will always remember.

YOUR COACHING PERSONA

Your conduct on and off the field will have a lasting impact on your players

Any good coach, regardless of the sport, is more than just a coach. The Xs and Os of any particular game are easy enough to teach, whether it is throwing a baseball, catching a football, or stopping a slap shot. What isn't always easy is gaining someone's trust.

As a coach, your duties extend far beyond what most people ever imagine. While your primary responsibilities are to teach the members of your team how to play a sport, you must remember that you are also molding young men and women. There are countless cases of people in all walks of life, all professions, all ages, all nationalities and genders who point to coaches they've encountered and the tremendous

A Plan of Action

- Determine a plan of action early in terms of your style and try to stick with it. If you're going to be strict, then be consistent. Be strict and apply the rules you set forth to everyone equally.

- Don't play favorites. Children with outgoing personalities or players with greater ability can curry favor with a coach simply by being who they are.

- Identify these players early and treat them as you would the quiet child or the one with less talent.

Smile

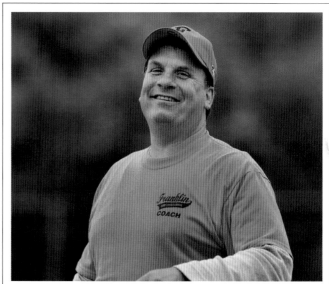

- Smile. It's that simple. Make the players feel welcome and wanted around you.

- You are a role model. Your behavior and expressions are easily read and copied by impressionable youngsters.

- Don't make faces when a player makes a bad play or struggles at the plate. This can be interpreted as mocking and the children will notice.

- Learn what each player's tolerance is for joking. Sometimes a good laugh can break tension.

impact these men and women have had on their lives.

No one is asking you to be a parent to these children. Rather, you are an extension of their parents and as such have a tremendous responsibility. You are trusted not only to teach these children how to play a game but to take care of them physically and mentally as well. Remember that a child is a parent's most precious commodity and for several hours a week they are handing this commodity over to you to mold and nurture.

Take great pride in this because not everyone is cut out to be a coach. Get to know your players and get to know their parents. You may not see some of them ever again once the season has ended. Others may become lifelong friends. In either case, know that these children have walked away from their experience with you as better people first and better ballplayers second.

Coaching is a privilege; it's not a right. Never forget that and the relationship you build with your team will be a lasting one.

Conduct

- Conduct yourself in a professional manner. While this isn't a professional setting, you should have some degree of decorum. Understand the boundaries between a player and coach and take care not to cross them.

- Wear your uniform properly. Tuck in your shirt and have the hat facing forward. Set a good example so that your team will look like a team.

- Remember that children will emulate what you do.

Having Fun

- Remember that this is all supposed to be fun. Most young players dream that they will someday play professional. Nurture that dream and encourage it regardless of the player's ability. Time will eventually level the playing field; there's no need for you to do it.

- Keep the stress levels low. Don't put pressure on the players, particularly the younger ones, to get the big hit or record the timely strikeout. They put enough pressure on themselves and are looking to you for support.

TALKING TO THE PARENTS
Winning over the parents is as important as gaining the trust of the players

Getting to know the parents of your players can be a delicate situation. Often, parents have trouble looking at their children objectively and are unable to see their limitations as a non-partial third party would. Parents also have, at times, trouble seeing just how good their son or daughter can be at whatever task they undertake, whether they are participating in sports, music, dance, etc. So if you're up for walking this tightrope, then get to it. Listen to what every parent has to say about her child and make a note of it. Not only is that the respectful thing to do, it may come in handy sometime in the future when you have to deal with a particular child.

Parents are not the enemy. You will find that many parents

Honesty

- Be honest with the parents. Let them know what you expect from them and their children.

- Remind them that you are making a commitment to their children as individuals and to the team as a group.

- You expect nothing less from them.

- There can be no secrets. If there is anything a parent needs to share with you about her child, have her do it now and not later.

You Are the Coach

- Remind the parents that you are the coach and while you would welcome any input from them privately on how to deal with their children, during games and practices you are in charge.

- Ask the parents not to shout out instructions from the stands or from behind the backstop. If too many people are instructing a youngster, confusion can ensue.

- Ask for their trust. You're coaching for a reason and can help their children. •

are simply willing to stay in the background and let you do your job. You are, after all, the coach. If you make the effort early enough in the relationship to understand any concerns a parent may have, it will be easier for you and the child.

Encouragement

- Remind the parents to encourage their child regardless of the child's performance.

- Children thrive on positive feedback. A pat on the back, a smile, or even a high five can take a potentially discouraging situation such as an error or a strikeout and make it better.

- Never stop giving encouragement. The players must know that you have confidence in their abilities regardless of the level on which they play.

Sportsmanship

- Stress to the players and the parents that being a good sport, above all else, is paramount to having a successful team.

- There is no "I" in team. Let the players know they win as one and they lose as one. It's a lesson that will serve them well their entire lives.

- Individual success is secondary to the needs of the team. Parents need to understand this concept as much if not more so than the players do.

MEET YOUR TEAM

The initial meeting between the coach and players can set the tone for the season

The initial meeting between a coach and his players is the sizing up period. You're watching them, they're watching you, and none of the involved parties has any idea what the next few months will involve.

It's your job as a coach to present them with that information at this meeting. Let them know about you and encourage them to ask questions. Ask questions of them and push them to ask questions of each other. You are, after all, going to be a family of sorts for several months, and if you start off the relationship in a positive manner then the chances of having problems in the future will greatly diminish.

Let the players and their families know who the assistant

The Get-together

- Sit your team in the dugout or in the stands. Have the players spend a few minutes with each other. Chances are many of them are already friends from school or the neighborhood.

- Observe if any of them are already friends. See whether certain players gravitate toward one another and attempt to determine if there are any cliques in the group.

- Let this occur naturally. Don't force anyone to sit or stand where they don't want to.

Background

- Give the team and the parents some background information about yourself. Let them know how long you've been coaching, where you went to school, whether you have any children, etc.

- Let them know if you played ball professionally or in college. Don't be humble when it comes to this. It will only enhance your credibility if the players and their parents understand you have an in-depth knowledge of the game.

- *Do not lie about yourself.* If you're caught in a lie, you will lose credibility and the trust of the team.

coaches will be and encourage those coaches to get involved in this meeting as well. You have a staff and that staff is an extension of you. Therefore, what they say and how they conduct themselves is a reflection on you.

Lay out your ground rules during this meeting. If you are open, honest, and up front right from the outset, then there should be no worries about players getting out of line as the season progresses. Tell players what is expected of them and ask what they expect of you. This two-way discussion should not only answer any questions anyone has but it should

also help create a foundation of trust between you and your players.

If they know that you are seeking their opinion or input about certain situations, they will have greater respect for you than if you simply barked orders and didn't listen when they spoke. This is your team and it's not a democracy. But there's no reason to make it a heavy-handed dictatorship, either.

The Introductions

- Have each player stand up, introduce himself, and share some information about who he is and why he wants to play baseball.

- Have the player address the team as well as you. Ask him and his parents several questions and have the other players follow suit. You want to know as much about the players as possible in order to do as much good as you can as a coach and mentor.

The Unit

- Stress as early and as often as possible that you are all there together to learn about working as a unit. They are now part of a team and their actions impact everyone, not just themselves.

- Discuss looking out for one another. If a player has a helpful suggestion or wishes to offer another player assistance, let him. These actions emphasize the team concept and teach compassion.

- Explain that there will be no room for whining or jealousy of other players.

5

FEMALE COACHES & TEAMMATES
Baseball is a sport that can be enjoyed by both men and women

The idea that baseball is a game for only men and boys is archaic. Women and girls have loved baseball for decades, so it's only natural that they would serve as players and coaches. Stories of female players, whether they formed their own league or tried to compete against the men, are not just the stuff of Hollywood scripts. Look no further than the All-American Girls Professional Baseball League that was formed during World War II.

Hundreds of Little League teams around the country have female coaches who serve as wonderful teachers and role models, not only for the young women on their teams but for the young men as well. Women can understand the nuances of baseball as well as men can.

Whether it is in the announcer's booth in New York or the front office in Los Angeles, women have become an accepted and integral part of the game. The notion that a

A Universal Game

- Explain that baseball is a game for everyone. Anyone can love and play the game, be it a man, woman, boy, or girl.

- Provide examples of how women have impacted the game of baseball by pointing out that there is a female broadcaster for the Yankees and a female assistant general manager for the Dodgers.

- Talk about how women have been honored by baseball, including getting their own exhibit at the National Baseball Hall of Fame and Museum in Cooperstown, New York.

Respect the Coach

- Female coaches are to be respected in the same fashion that you would respect a male coach. Coarse language and rude behavior will not be tolerated.

- Any displays of disrespect to a female coach or player will be dealt with quickly and, if warranted, severely.

That includes being asked to leave the field or sitting out a game.

- Discuss with the parents that female coaches are on your staff and what is expected of the players in terms of respect.

player couldn't learn from a female coach is outdated and ignorant in today's world. A person's gender does not in any way impede his or her ability to learn or teach.

While girls and boys will eventually have to part at some point during their development because of age and physical differences, the lessons learned by playing alongside female ballplayers far outweigh any stereotypical negatives that could arise.

Respect Your Teammates

- Ask the boys to treat their female teammates with the same respect they would treat male teammates. While they are their equals on the field, they should not smack, tackle, grab, or roughhouse with them. They are young women; treat them as such.

- Conversely, female players should not expect special treatment from women coaches or simply because they are girls.

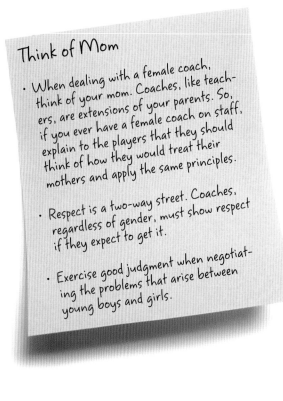

Think of Mom

- When dealing with a female coach, think of your mom. Coaches, like teachers, are extensions of your parents. So, if you ever have a female coach on staff, explain to the players that they should think of how they would treat their mothers and apply the same principles.

- Respect is a two-way street. Coaches, regardless of gender, must show respect if they expect to get it.

- Exercise good judgment when negotiating the problems that arise between young boys and girls.

ACCEPTABLE BALL FIELD BEHAVIOR

There are certain ways to act on the baseball field, in the dugout, and in the stands

There is more to learning about baseball than throwing a ball or swinging a bat. There are life lessons to be taught when experiencing the game, lessons that are valuable and could serve the youngsters throughout their lives.

The opportunity to help mold young men and women is never greater than in the relationship between a coach and a player. We've talked about how youngsters emulate adults, especially authority figures, so this is the perfect opportunity for you as a coach to do some genuine good. Simply imagine how you would want the players on your team to act and then behave that way yourself.

If you're not screaming at the umpire or cursing in the

Temper, Temper

- Explain that there will be no displays of temper on the field. This includes shouting at coaches or teammates. Disrespectful behavior is unacceptable.

- As a coach, you must also control your temper. Set a good example for your team by not screaming at the players, other coaches, or parents.

- Try not to argue with the umpire, particularly at the younger levels. The consequences of the games aren't so great that an argument is needed. Let the players know that you will deal with the umpire.

Don't Lose Control

- Let the players know that there will be no throwing of equipment. Their equipment—bats, gloves, etc.—are their tools, and for them to become better ballplayers, they must take care of their tools.

- Be firm when telling the players that they cannot touch their teammates or the opposing players. There is no room for violence in baseball, particularly where children are concerned.

- Go cool off. Let the players know it is acceptable to walk away for a few seconds, collect their thoughts, and calm down.

dugout, then odds are the team won't be, either. If you're not mocking your players or putting them down when they make a poor play or strike out, odds are the team won't either.

Show them how to act. This is the part of the game in which you can receive your greatest gift as a teacher. Be congratulatory when something is done well and conciliatory when something is done poorly. This teaches compassion and respect and instills a sense of camaraderie amongst the players.

Be sure that the parents are aware of your thoughts on the subject. Let them know that there will be no room for screaming at the players, whether it's the players on their child's team or the opposition. Stress that you will ask them to leave the field unless they can conduct themselves properly.

An embarrassing parent can be as harmful to a child's psyche as a tormentor in his own grade. Make the parents aware of this before the season starts, and mention it prior to every game if you feel it is necessary.

Watch the Language

- Inform your players that there will be no cursing at or teasing of teammates or opposing players.

- While all the children on your team may not be friends with each of their teammates, instruct them that they should respect everyone on the team and treat them the way that they would like to be treated.

- There is no room for racial, gender-based, or off-color remarks. Such comments should be dealt with quickly and with the help of a parent.

Sportsmanship

- Be a good sport. When you win, be humble in victory. When you lose, hold your head high.

- Be sure your team shakes hands with the players on the opposite team, win or lose.

- Stress to your team that winning and losing are important but not nearly as important as being an honorable young man or woman.

- Do not cheat. No one likes a cheater or the advantage he gains by being dishonest.

9

BE PREPARED

Be ready for any situation when preparing to play or practice

The Boy Scout motto is a good one to have handy when talking about baseball. Often young children lack the focus needed to do anything that involves a great deal of preparation regardless of how bright they are. This includes preparing to play baseball.

Don't be afraid to repeat yourself. Make up mantras if you must but continually stress how important it is for your players to be prepared. Constantly remind them to bring their equipment with them to practice and take it home with them when the day is done. Ask any parent that has small children about having to repeat himself and the answer will almost always be the same—it has to be done.

While you may tell the team what to do a thousand times, the first time you don't remind them about something will be the time that a player will forget to bring a hat or a glove or fail to bring it home. So be patient with them. They are

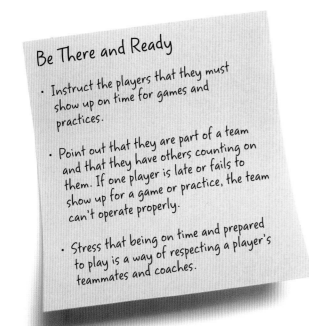

Be There and Ready

- Instruct the players that they must show up on time for games and practices.

- Point out that they are part of a team and that they have others counting on them. If one player is late or fails to show up for a game or practice, the team can't operate properly.

- Stress that being on time and prepared to play is a way of respecting a player's teammates and coaches.

Remember Your Equipment

Player Checklist
Glove
Bat
Cleats
Hat
Equipment Bag
Water

- Remind your players that it is imperative to never forget any of their equipment when coming to a game or practice.

- Continue to hammer home the point about bringing their gloves, bats, and hats while always wearing their spikes. Remember to tell everyone to take their equipment home.

- Remind them that preparing to play involves taking care of their equipment, whether it's oiling their gloves or cleaning their spikes.

little people; don't forget that. While an adult would view bringing their equipment to a baseball game as common sense, children, particularly those under the age of ten, aren't always as reasonable.

Also, remind them early and often that they have to be prepared to play when they arrive at the field. Practice and games start at specific times so there is little room for goofing around. If they want to chase their friends around the outfield or build castles with the infield dirt, then that's something they can do on their own time.

Once they have arrived at the baseball field, you shouldn't have to raise your voice to get them together or get their attention. Set a routine from Day One and stick to it. If you're prepared, they will be, too.

Drink

- Stress to the players and their parents that they should bring plenty of water to every game, regardless of the temperature.

- As the weather gets warmer, dehydration could become a problem.

- Be sure the players drink plenty of fluids in between innings, particularly during warmer days. In addition to dehydration, a player can develop cramps from a lack of fluids.

- If a player feels sick, send him to his parents.

Think

- Think before you act. It's a wonderful practice in which to engage and one that is particularly useful on the baseball field.

- Preach to your players that they should think about what they're going to do if the ball is hit to them.

- Stress to every one of them that they need to think about how to approach their turn at bat.

- Be sure they are aware of the proper behavior when sitting in the dugout and the consequences for inappropriate conduct.

GLOVES

The proper glove can make the difference between an average fielder and an exceptional one

Imagine a carpenter trying to build a house without the proper set of tools. What would the building look like if he only had a hacksaw to cut the wood? How do you think he would make out if he had only a Phillips screwdriver and not a regular one? Would he be able to hammer nails without a hammer?

You get the point. The tools of your trade are very important in terms of doing your job properly. Without them, getting the job done is difficult if not impossible. The glove, regardless of what position you play, is one of the most important tools a player has.

Helping your players choose their gloves is of paramount

The First Baseman's Glove

- The first baseman's glove generally lacks fingers.

- Larger than regular gloves, a first baseman's mitt cannot be longer than 12 inches from top to bottom and 8 inches wide. The webbing can be no larger than 5 inches from the top to the base.

- Most first baseman's mitts are made for left-handed fielders.

- The webbing is a bit more flexible so the first baseman can receive the throw without worrying about the ball bouncing out of his glove.

The Outfielder's Glove

- An outfielder's glove is usually longer than the infielder's gloves.

- The outfielder is less likely to lose a ball because the extra size and deeper pocket allow him to extend his hand farther for the ball while making a diving or running catch.

- The size of the glove is a result of personal taste and preference, but by rule the glove cannot be larger than 12 inches from top to bottom.

importance. It can't be too big and it can't be too small. It has to be just right. It has to fit comfortably on the hand but it can't be too tight. It can't be too loose either because it will fall off, especially when attempting to field a hard-hit ball.

Remind your players that they should take their time when choosing a glove. This particular piece of equipment is an extension of their bodies and, if taken care of properly, can last for years.

The Infielder's Glove

- Smaller is better. The glove should be smaller than an outfielder's glove and form fitting as if it were an extension of the player's hand.

- Players should avoid wearing a batting glove under the infielder's glove. The glove should fit snugly and mold to the bare hand.

- Gloves with wider pockets will allow for more room when fielding a ground ball.

- Instruct players to keep all fingers inside the glove for maximum feel and to prevent injury.

Oiling and Glove Care

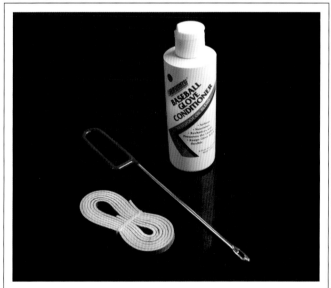

- Liberally use glove oil and apply evenly over the entire surface without saturating the leather.

- Place a baseball inside the pocket, close the glove, and tie it tightly. An old sock is the wrap of choice.

- Always try to have a leather-working kit handy. You never know when you'll have to restring or repair a player's glove. Practice on an old glove if one is available to get the feel of working with the leather.

BATS

Choosing the correct piece of lumber—or aluminum—takes time, patience, and knowledge

Choosing a bat is a great deal like choosing a glove. Bigger doesn't always mean better. It just means more cumbersome. So when choosing a bat for one of your players, consider the player's weight, size, strength, and ability regardless of whether the bat you're selecting is made of wood, aluminum, or composite.

If a bat is too big for a youngster, she won't be able to swing it. It's that simple. If it's too small, they'll be swinging too fast or not making contact, which leads to another set of problems. Generally, younger children don't need much more than a 28-ounce bat.

There are exceptions for the child who is bigger, stronger,

KNACK COACHING YOUTH BASEBALL

The Aluminum/Composite Bat

- Though aluminum bats break on occasion or "go dead" from time to time, they remain cheaper alternatives to wood.

- A ball that is hit by an aluminum bat travels farther and faster than a ball hit with wood.

- Thinner aluminum allows for a lighter bat with a larger sweet spot and more of a spring or trampoline effect when the ball explodes off the bat.

- Composite bats consistently outperform aluminum bats.

The Wooden Bat

- Professional players are only allowed to use wooden bats.

- Players should keep their bats clean and wipe them down with rubbing alcohol after each game or practice.

- Make sure players work the handle well with the alcohol. Pine tar can accumulate and as a result dirt can build up.

- Roll a wood bat with another wood bat or a piece of bone. This will keep the wood smooth and prevent any possible cracks or fissures from developing.

or far more talented. But those cases are few and far between until you reach the early teen years.

When helping a player select a bat, stress that the speed at which the bat travels through the hitting zone is more important than the size of the bat he's swinging. If your player has the proper bat, he will generate the necessary bat speed to produce solid contact. If the bat is too heavy, it will drag through the strike zone.

EQUIPMENT

The Fungo Bat

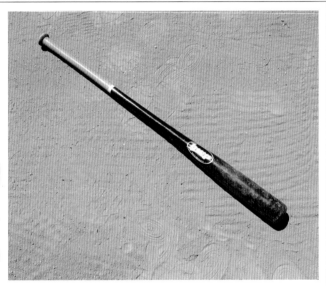

- Fungo bats are longer, lighter, and thinner than regular bats and are used for practice purposes.

- Fungo bats are usually 35 to 37 inches long and no more than 22 ounces.

- The smaller size makes it easier to hit popups.

- When hitting balls with the fungo bat, it is easier to hit flies when the ball is at shoulder level. Hit grounders when the ball is at chest level.

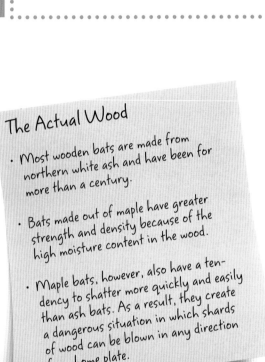

The Actual Wood

- Most wooden bats are made from northern white ash and have been for more than a century.

- Bats made out of maple have greater strength and density because of the high moisture content in the wood.

- Maple bats, however, also have a tendency to shatter more quickly and easily than ash bats. As a result, they create a dangerous situation in which shards of wood can be blown in any direction from home plate.

CATCHING EQUIPMENT

Equipment used by the catcher is the most important in the game

A catcher's equipment is known as the "tools of ignorance" in baseball, and with good reason. It takes courage and skill to get behind the plate, and you'd have to be a fool to go back there without protection, making the phrase a bit ironic. Muddy Ruel, a wonderful backstop who caught Hall of Famer Walter Johnson in the 1920s, is credited with coining the now famous saying.

This is the most dangerous of positions, one that can end careers quickly. However, today's state-of-the-art equipment can go a long way in preventing many injuries that would otherwise occur on a daily basis. Think about how many times a catcher is hit with a foul ball in the knees, the chest, or off the facemask during the course of the game.

While these hits can often leave a catcher shaken, they rarely force him to leave the game because of the quality of the equipment. Imagine the severity of the injury had the

The Shinguards

- The shinguards are made of leather, padding, and heavy-duty plastic or composite material.

- They should fit snugly on the legs while still providing mobility and flexibility. If the shinguards are too loose, they may slip or move, leaving an area of the kneecap or shin exposed to potential foul balls.

- Many sets of shinguards have extensions that cover the top of the foot and the toes.

The Mask/Helmet

- There are two types of masks: the traditional over-the-helmet facemask and the hockey-style goalie mask and helmet.

- Be sure the mask has good sight lines and does not block any of the catcher's field of vision.

- It is important that the mask fit snugly. If it is too loose, it can slip and serious injury can occur.

- Most masks/helmets have an optional throat guard that hangs down several inches to cover the exposed Adam's apple. It is highly recommended.

catcher not been wearing the mask, helmet, or shinguards. Providing your players with the proper equipment and making sure that it is maintained and safe will prevent injuries both severe and small.

The Chest Protector

- Be sure the chest protector fits tightly but not to a point where it encroaches on movement. It needs to cover the torso from the waist to the throat.

- Some chest protectors come with optional shoulder guards that can be removed. The shoulder guards are generally worn on the non-throwing shoulder.

- One style of chest protector offers a flap that extends down to cover the groin.

The Glove

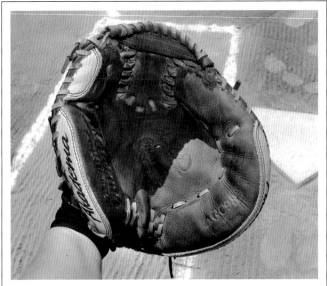

- The single-break glove is the most common and popular glove used by catchers today.

- Larger catcher's mitts are available for catching knuckleball pitchers.

- The glove may be no more than 38 inches in circumference and no more than 15½ from wrist to fingertips.

- The space between the thumb section and the finger section can't be more than 6 inches at the top of the glove or 4 inches at the base.

UNIFORM
Players show respect by taking care of their uniforms

Uniforms are to be worn with pride. Whether you're coaching the Marlins or Mets, the Dodgers or Diamondbacks, tell players to be proud of the team for which they play. When they are wearing the uniform, it makes them part of a team, part of something special: Individuality ceases to exist. Each player is part of a unit, and the uniform and cap represent that unit.

Let your players know that wearing the team colors is a privilege, not a right. It is what distinguishes them from every other team in the league. While this may come across as a rah-rah speech, it is important for the players to identify with their team. Remind them that it is special to be a Yankee or a Blue Jay and that the uniform they are wearing lets everyone know how special they are. Make a big deal about the uniform and caring for it, treating it with respect. It's a valuable lesson that will serve your players well.

Socks and Stirrups

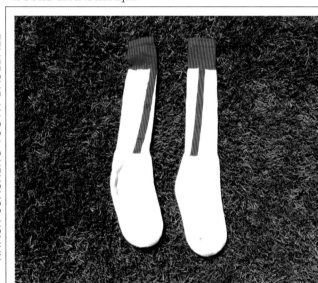

- The socks worn by baseball players are generally white.

- The stirrup is a colored sock worn over the white sock that has no bottom, only a thin piece of material that fits over the heel and is held in place by a player's spikes.

- Many players today have abandoned the stirrups in favor of a dual-colored sock that gives the appearance of a stirrup.

- It is a popular practice to wear the uniform pants so low that the socks aren't even visible.

Spikes

- When looking to purchase spikes, players should employ the same methods they would use when searching for a pair of regular shoes or sneakers. They need to be comfortable and broken in before being used in game situations.

- Attachments to the heel or toe that could cause injury to an opposing player are not permitted.

- Pointed spikes, like those worn by golfers or runners, can cause serious injuries to the opposition and are not permitted.

ZOOM

Hall of Fame owner and legendary promoter Bill Veeck actually had his Chicago White Sox wear uniform shorts and kneesocks in the first game of a doubleheader against Kansas City on August 9, 1976. The ugly and embarrassing uniforms were used only once, but the White Sox won the game, 5–2.

Team Uniform and Cap

- Players should wash and dry the uniform properly after every game.

- All players should wear identical uniforms in trim and style with no individual alterations or variations.

- Be sure each uniform fits properly. If it is too big or too small, it could impede the player's ability to perform.

- Players should wear caps facing forward without stickers or tags when on the field out of respect for the game and their teammates.

Protective Cup

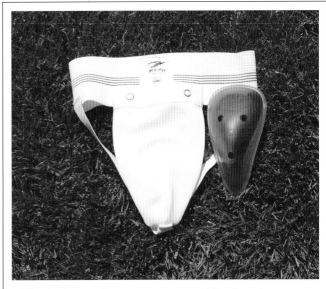

- The single most important piece of equipment a baseball player owns, the protective cup should be worn at all times on the baseball field.

- The cup, which is made of heavy-duty plastic, should provide adequate coverage without causing chafing or irritation.

- The cup fits into a pouch that is suspended from an elastic waistband or placed inside a pair of form-fitting pants called sliders.

HELMETS & PROTECTIVE EQUIPMENT
Protecting the body is often an overlooked part of playing baseball

There are not many pieces of protective equipment to discuss when talking about baseball. It's not like football or hockey where every player must be protected to the fullest in order to avoid injury. Baseball has its protective gear as well, but most of it is limited to the catcher and what the batter brings with him to the plate.

Here's a closer look at the types of protective equipment used by most batters and the occasional fielder.

Remember that baseball is largely a game based on confidence. *See the ball, hit the ball, catch the ball* is a wonderfully simple mantra employed by thousands of coaches and managers for more than one hundred years. That mantra, however, isn't so simple if you play scared or if you worry about getting hurt.

Some of the equipment we will discuss is designed to allay those fears. Elbow pads, face shields, and heart guards are

Helmets

- Be sure the helmet fits properly. If it's too big, it will slide or slip and hinder the batter's ability to see the incoming pitch.

- Helmets with earflaps are mandatory.

- Some helmets for younger players come with chin straps. The chin strap, however, isn't necessary if the helmet fits properly.

- Helmets must be worn while on the bases, when in the on-deck circle, and on the coaching lines. Helmets for adults coaching the bases are optional but highly recommended.

Faceguards

- Helmets with faceguards are available and can cost as much as $75. Faceguards can be purchased separately for much less.

- While faceguards are a good idea to help protect a player coming back from an injury, such as a broken cheek or nose, wearing one as a matter of course is not recommended.

- Faceguards can impede vision and affect confidence at the plate.

available to prevent injury and all work to some degree. The best way to prevent injury, however, is to simply play with abandon at every moment and give 100 percent effort. If you spend too much time worrying about getting hurt, chances are you will.

Surprisingly, batting helmets were not made mandatory in baseball until the early 1970s. Several players had been severely injured and one—Ray Chapman—had even died, yet it took decades for helmets to come into vogue. Batting helmets with earflaps were made mandatory for all incoming Major League players in the early 1980s.

Elbow Pads

- Major Leaguers brought these pads into vogue in the last ten to fifteen years as a result of their propensity to crowd the plate while batting.

- Elbow pads will provide protection and confidence if an opposing pitcher likes to pitch inside.

- Putting pads on younger players, though, can impede the swing.

- Most of the pads are lightweight and made of a combination of foam, plastic, and Velcro.

Heart Guard Shirts

- There is some controversy about whether the heart guard actually does any good.

- The piece of plastic that is sewn into the shirt is designed to absorb the blow of a line drive to the chest.

- There are some experts who believe that the guard itself does little to diffuse the impact of a line drive.

- After wearing the heart guard for several games, most children report that they aren't even aware of its presence.

BALLS
You can't play baseball without the baseball

Well, that's not entirely true. Children worldwide have been playing baseball for generations with some old rags and a little duct tape. It is amazing how creative a child can be when it comes to figuring out what to use as a baseball. While that creativity gets the job done, nothing works as well as that little, leather-covered sphere.

The baseball hasn't gone through many changes in the last one hundred or so years, though some believe that the "dead-ball era" that ended with the emergence of Babe Ruth was as much a result of a newer, juiced-up baseball as it was anything that The Bambino did.

In reality, teams simply stopped using baseballs until they were almost rags. New balls were introduced into the game at a greater pace, particularly when they got dirty, and this helped contribute to the offensive boom and The Babe's success. While the ball has undergone some subtle changes

Soft Baseball

- A soft baseball is made to the specifications of a regulation baseball.

- A soft baseball looks like a normal baseball but is spongy to the touch.

- These balls are designed for younger children, ages five through seven. It allows them to get the feel of holding a baseball and playing with it without subjecting them to the dangers of playing with a hard ball.

Hard Baseball

- Regulation baseballs are made to specific Major League Baseball standards.

- The ball is made of yarn wound tightly around a small ball of cork, rubber, or similar material.

- There are two strips of white horsehide or cowhide stitched tightly together.

- Balls cannot weigh less than 5 ounces or more than 5¼ ounces. They can be no smaller than 9 inches in diameter and no larger than 9¼ inches around.

over the years—the yarn is wrapped much tighter around the cork core than it once was—the look and feel has essentially remained the same since the game took off in popularity in the early twentieth century.

EQUIPMENT

Softball

- A softball is essentially a larger version of a baseball.

- It is made with cork, yarn, and leather, the same as a baseball.

- The size and weight of a softball can vary from association to association. The rules that govern international play call for a 12-inch ball with a weight of 6¼ to 7 ounces.

- An 11-inch ball can weigh between 5⅞ ounces and 6⅛ ounces.

Rubber/Batting Cage Baseballs

- There are many different designs for batting cage baseballs, all of which are geared toward durability.

- These balls can cost anywhere from $30 to $45 a dozen, depending on the style and brand purchased.

- A popular version is the dimpled ball that resembles a large golf ball.

- Specialty balls can also be used. These balls are hard foam balls that come in the shape of baseballs or Wiffle balls that can be used in batting and pitching practice.

POSITIONS

Each of the nine positions on the field is important for its own reasons

When you are coaching youngsters, do not assume that they are knowledgeable about the game's most basic fundamentals simply because they have stepped onto the baseball field. Ask a seven-year-old to go play second base and watch how many times he will actually go stand on second base rather than move to the position on the field where the second baseman traditionally plays.

It is your job as the coach to be a teacher. While many children will learn the basics of the game from their parents, who learned them from their parents and so on, there are just as many young players who have no idea about the simplest points involving the game. It is your job to instruct them in

The Infield

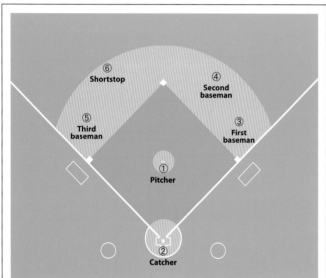

- The infield is composed of four position players—the first baseman, the second baseman, the third baseman, and the shortstop. All must play in fair territory, inside the foul lines.

- The first baseman is abbreviated 1B and positioned as 3 on the scorecard.

- The second baseman is abbreviated 2B and positioned as 4 on the scorecard.

- The third baseman is abbreviated 3B and positioned as 5 on the scorecard.

- The shortstop is abbreviated as SS and positioned as 6 on the scorecard.

The Outfield

- The outfield is composed of three position players—a left fielder, a center fielder, and a right fielder.

- The left fielder is abbreviated LF and positioned as 7 on the scorecard. The center fielder is abbreviated CF and positioned as 8 on the scorecard, while the right fielder is abbreviated RF and positioned as 9 on the scorecard.

- While the outfielders can position themselves wherever they like, they must also be in fair territory.

a manner that is not condescending or embarrassing. Lack of knowledge does not denote ignorance; it simply means something has yet to be learned.

Remind the more learned players, too, that not everyone is as immersed in the game as they are. They must be tolerant and patient with their teammates as they go through the learning process. Some children have parents that don't like or follow baseball, or are unfamiliar with the game. These are the children who need a little extra time and attention.

So pointing out what each of the positions is and where the players who occupy those positions generally play is a great way to begin any lesson. Ask your players questions about where each of the positions is located. If they aren't aware, walk them around the field and show them. It's a simple exercise that takes only a few minutes and will give the less knowledgeable players a chance to learn while reinforcing what the more experienced players already know.

The Pitcher

- The pitcher is abbreviated P and is positioned as 1 on the scorecard.

- The pitcher stands on the mound in the center of the infield and must start each play in contact with the pitching rubber on the mound.

- Pitchers can either be starters or relievers. Starters, as the name suggests, start the game and pitch as long or as little as the manager decides.

- There are several unofficial classifications of relievers—long reliever, middle reliever, setup man, and closer.

The Catcher

- The catcher is abbreviated as C and positioned as 2 on the scorecard.

- The catcher is positioned behind home plate and must begin every play in the box behind the plate.

- The catcher can step out of the box once the ball is pitched, either to grab a wild pitch or for an intentional walk.

- Catching requires a high degree of stamina because of the fatigue caused by playing the position.

THE FIELD

From cow pastures and cornfields to stadiums, the field remains a constant in baseball

When discussing the standard positions in baseball, the inevitable questions about the field will arise. While most youngsters will not be concerned about a field's dimensions, what the distance is in between bases, and whether or not the mound is too high or too low, you should be.

A coach has to know it all because sooner or later someone is going to ask, whether it's a player or parent. So be prepared and know the answers. Prepare your players as well. Being complete players means understanding all aspects of the game. While it is a thrill to learn about the physical and mental aspects of the game, learning about the aesthetics is also important.

The Bases

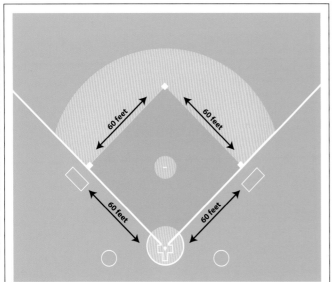

- There are three bases—first, second, and third—that are square, white bags made of anything from canvas and rubber to plastic. Home plate is made of hard rubber and is embedded in the ground.

- The distance between bases is 60 feet for most Little Leagues and youth softball leagues. As the players get older and reach high school age, the distance between the bases will mirror that of the Major Leagues—90 feet.

The Rubber to Home

- The distance between the rubber and home plate in most Little Leagues is 46 feet.

- As the players get older and reach high school age, the distance between the pitching rubber and home plate increases to the Major league distance of 60 feet, 6 inches.

- Softball leagues have a different set of rules and the distance between the rubber and home plate in these leagues can vary between 35 and 53 feet depending on the age of the players.

There are basic terms that are considered common knowledge. There are basic numbers—like the distance between home plate and the mound—that are also easily rattled off by baseball fans. It is these terms that should be discussed in order to make your players well rounded when it comes to discussing the game. They are children and are at a point in their lives when learning is a bit easier. Give them the information and be amazed at how much they absorb.

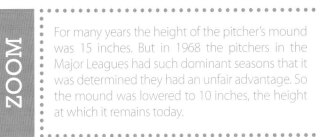

The Mound

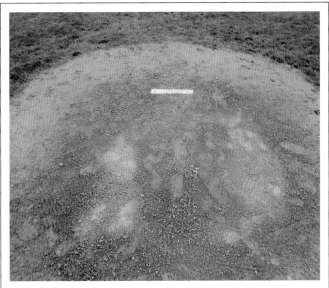

- The mound, as the name would suggest, is a sculpted pile of dirt in the middle of the infield.

- Atop the mound is the pitching rubber, which is elevated 10 inches above the rest of the field.

- Beginning 6 inches in front of the rubber, the mound begins to slope at a rate of 1 inch per foot for at least 6 feet.

- The pitcher's mound has a diameter of 18 feet, though some fields don't have actual mounds. The name, however, still applies.

The Warning Track

- The warning track is the area of dirt closest to the wall or the fence that surrounds the playing field.

- As the name would suggest, the track is designed to issue a warning to the players that they are approaching a wall or fence should they be running to catch a fly ball.

- It is believed that the term "warning track" originates from the actual running track that surrounded the field at the original Yankee Stadium.

BASERUNNING

Running the bases is an art form that requires practice and patience

Running the bases should be as simple as going from Point A to Point B, but rarely is it ever that easy. There is a great deal of thought required when it comes to running the bases. While the rules governing baserunning are not as in depth as some of the rules that apply to the rest of the game, they are still important enough to be discussed early and often.

The best way to discuss baserunning is to put it in terms of common sense. It doesn't take much for a player to figure out what to do once a ball has been put into play. It simply takes common sense. Where was the ball hit? Do I have enough time to advance an extra base? Will I be running my team out of an inning if I try to move up?

These are all common questions that are answered in greater detail in Chapter 19, which is dedicated solely to running the bases. The short version, however, is this: Instruct your players to think and pay attention after going over the

The Turn at First

- This play often confuses younger players. When running to first base, they should run through the bag and either stay straight or break into foul territory.

- The player should only make the turn to or take a step toward second base if he has intentions of going to second base.

- A runner can be tagged out if he turns toward second base because it is inferred that he is attempting to move up.

One Base, One Runner

- No two runners may occupy one base at the same time. The lead runner is entitled to the base.

- Be sure players pay attention to the play in front of them while running the bases. If a baserunner sees another runner slowing down or stopped, then he must slow down or stop and remain at the nearest base.

- If two runners do find themselves approaching the same base—one moving forward and one moving backward—one of the runners should initiate a rundown to give the other a chance to reach the base safely.

basic rules of running the bases. Quiz them often on the rules and drill them on how to perform when certain circumstances in the game arise.

Tagging Up

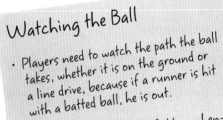

Watching the Ball

- Players need to watch the path the ball takes, whether it is on the ground or a line drive, because if a runner is hit with a batted ball, he is out.

- Avoid colliding with the fielders whenever possible. If the runner is deemed to have interfered with a fielder purposely, he will be called out and all other runners will return to the base they previously occupied.

- A runner cannot leave a base on a fly ball until the fielder has caught the ball.

- If a runner leaves the base before the ball is caught, he must return to the base and tag or risk being called out, either as part of a double play or in an appeal play.

- An appeal play occurs when the defensive player appeals to the umpire, suggesting that the runner left the base early and therefore should be called out.

BALLS & STRIKES

Knowing and understanding the strike zone is an important aspect of the game

Teach your players where the strike zone is. It should be one of the first things you do when working with players who are in a league where they are allowed to pitch.

While the size of the strike zone is always open for interpretation, the rules of the game don't leave much wiggle room. So find a piece of plywood, get some chalk or some paint, and draw the strike zone. Years ago, handball courts, schoolyard walls, and sides of buildings were dotted with strike-zone boxes.

They aren't seen much anymore and perhaps that is in direct correlation with many younger players not understanding the strike zone. Set up the example as best you

Balls and Strikes

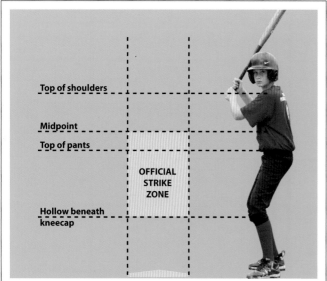

Top of shoulders

Midpoint

Top of pants

OFFICIAL STRIKE ZONE

Hollow beneath kneecap

- The strike zone is the area above home plate and by rule is between the armpit of the batter and his knees.

- Determining the strike zone is the umpire's decision based on whether he believes the batter is taking a natural stance at the plate.

- Umpires use their discretion to call balls and strikes and can sometimes make mistakes.

- Explain to your players what the strike zone is.

Foul Tips/Foul Balls

- A foul ball is any batted ball that lands in foul territory, out of play, or in the stands.

- A batted ball that hits an umpire, coach, bat boy, or player in the on-deck circle or any other object, such as a bat or ball bag, outside the lines is considered foul.

- A foul tip is a batted ball that goes directly to the catcher and is caught.

- A foul tip on a third strike must be caught for the strikeout to be complete.

can and let them practice throwing at it. It's the simplest and most direct way for them to become familiar with the accepted strike zone.

Stress to your players, though, that arguing balls and strikes is a no-no. Children shouldn't be arguing with the umpire about whether or not a ball was over the plate, mostly because they probably aren't even aware themselves where the ball crossed the plate. Set a good example.

Do not argue about balls and strikes. Rather, quietly and casually speak to the umpire after the inning has ended. Not only will it show your respect for the umpire but it will also set a good example. If your players see you arguing with the umpire, it will prompt them to do the same. Instruct the parents of your players to be quiet as well. Catcalls and chirping at the umpires from the stands will serve as a prompt for the players to do the same.

Intentional Walks

- Stronger hitters may be given an intentional walk. Four balls are purposely thrown out of the strike zone, away from the plate with the catcher standing to receive them.

- The four pitches must be thrown. An umpire cannot simply allow a player to take first base.

- Make sure the catcher and the pitcher are in agreement about an intentional walk before a pitcher throws a ball outside; otherwise it could be a wild pitch and any runners could advance.

The Balk

- Defined as an illegal act by the pitcher, allowing the runners to advance a base.

- There are thirteen actions that can provoke a balk call. The most common are making a pickoff throw to a base without stepping toward that base and not coming to a complete stop while throwing a pitch from the set position.

- Balks are no longer called in any division of Little League but are a part of pitching that needs to be taught.

UMPIRES

Understanding and respecting the men in blue makes the game easier and more enjoyable

Umpires have a job to do. Your job is to coach. The players are there to play. The umpires are there to keep order.

Now, we're not saying that anarchy would ensue if there were no umpires at a baseball game—though when dealing with youngsters, you never know. Umpires do keep the chaos factor out of the game while allowing the coaches and

players to do what they do best. Without them, there would be no game because an umpire is involved in every single pitch and every single play.

The same can't be said about any other sport. Plays can be run in football and if there are no penalties called, the referees are bystanders. The action in basketball and hockey

Positioning of the Umpires

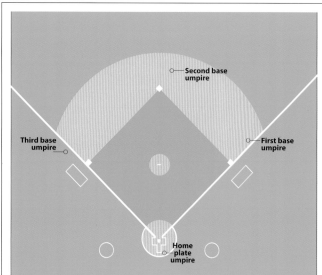

Second base umpire

Third base umpire

First base umpire

Home plate umpire

- Major League Baseball games require four umpires—one for every base. During All-Star games as well as playoff and World Series games, there are also umpires down each foul line.

- Little League games often have only one or two

umpires depending on availability. If there are two umpires, one is stationed behind home plate while the field umpire is at first base.

- Often, if there is only one umpire, he can stand behind the pitcher's mound and officiate the entire game from there.

Umpiring Tasks

- The umpire's job is to enforce the rules. He must have a detailed knowledge of the rule book and be able to use that knowledge to make a call in any given situation.

- The home-plate umpire calls balls and strikes in addition to making calls at the plate.

- Base umpires make the calls at their respective bases but can ask for help from other umpires when making a call.

games can go on for minutes at a time without the referees ever getting involved. But in baseball, every pitch is called a ball or a strike. If a player hits a fly ball that is caught, he's signaled out. If a player hits a grounder and the fielder makes a throw, he's either signaled out or safe by the umpire. The umpire can even call a batter safe on a base hit.

Umpires are there for a very important reason. Respect them and respect their work. Do not argue or be rude to the umpire. Do not provoke him or look for an argument. He is the police officer on the field, keeping order and enforcing the rules. If you as a coach subscribe to that notion, then your players will as well.

Stress the idea early and often that being disrespectful to the umpire will not be tolerated. Then back up your words with actions and treat the umps well. It will only make for a better game and better time for everyone involved.

Respecting the Umpire

- The umpire is the authority figure on the field. If you show him respect, your players will as well.

- The umpire's decision is usually final. If you think he has made an error, ask him to consult the other umpires. Remember, though, he is under no obligation to do so.

- There can be no talking back to or cursing at the umpire. Keep your temper in check.

Reading the Umpire

- If you have been coaching in your respective league for several seasons, you probably have a good idea of how certain umpires behave.

- Study an umpire's strike zone and pass that information on to your players.

- Pay close attention to an umpire's tolerance threshold. Know how far you can push him but always be respectful and cajoling.

- It is better to say nothing than to be a smart aleck with the umpire.

GENERAL FIELDING RULES
Knowing some of the basic rules about what you can and can't do is important

It would be almost impossible as a coach to know every rule down to every last detail in the book. Therefore, it would be completely impossible for a child to memorize all the rules and regulations that go along with playing baseball.

As a coach, it is up to you to give the players a brief overview of some of the more important rules and situations that can come into play frequently during the course of a game. While some of the plays we will discuss in this section could actually turn out to be cute—youngsters running out of the basepaths trying to avoid a tag is always a favorite—it is important that your players learn early on what is and what is not acceptable when it comes to being on the field.

Obstruction

KNACK COACHING YOUTH BASEBALL

The Neighborhood Play

- This occurs when a player—usually the second baseman or the shortstop—drifts over the base or near it, implying that he has touched the base while turning a double play though he was not actually on the base when in possession of the ball.

- The neighborhood play is a generally accepted part of the game, one that is usually never called unless the umpire is a complete stickler for the rules.

- This occurs when a fielder who does not have possession of the ball prohibits the runner from advancing.

- The fielder who does not have the ball is required to stay out of the runner's line to the base.

- A player cannot block a base without the ball. While waiting for the throw, the fielder must not impede the runner's ability to arrive at the base before he has possession of the ball.

These are the types of plays and rules that don't occur with great frequency. But when they do occur, they can have a great impact on the outcome of the game. Imagine losing a game by a run because your second baseman didn't know enough to get out of a runner's way on a play that would have ended an inning. There are so many little subtleties involved in the game. Pick a new one every day and discuss it with your team.

Fielding Foul Balls

- Once a ball has landed in foul territory via a bunt or popup, a player should grab it.

- A ball that lands in foul territory before first or third base can be called fair if it bounces back into fair territory before it is touched.

- Teach players to be aware of baserunners when fielding foul balls. Runners are allowed to tag up on fly balls that are caught in foul territory.

Foot on the Base

- When accepting the throw for a force play or at first base, the player's foot must touch the base. It does not have to be directly on top of the base. In fact, it is dangerous to have your foot on the base in such a manner because it can lead to serious injury.

- The player should place his foot alongside the base so that it is resting against it, either in a parallel fashion or with the heel touching the base.

35

STRETCHING
Stretching out muscles can prevent injuries

A baseball player's legs are his foundation for a strong performance. Without strong, healthy, properly stretched and developed legs, pitchers have no drive to push off the mound properly. Hitters face the same problem. Without stretched and strong legs, they won't be able to drive the baseball and will be forced to use their upper torso more. This puts a strain on the upper body and could lead to more injuries.

From a fielding standpoint, you can't run or field the position properly if your legs are too stiff to allow fluid movement. And baserunning? Well, that will be a problem, too. If a youngster tries to run too much or too quickly without having stretched out his legs properly, he can pull a hamstring, quadriceps, calf, or groin muscle very easily. These injuries can be very painful and can keep him off the field for a prolonged period of time.

A pulled hamstring can be particularly devastating. There

The Right Leg Muscles

- Have players stand straight with their feet apart at shoulder width, arms at their sides.

- Ask each player to pull his right leg up behind him with his right arm, bending it at the knee, holding his foot as close to the buttocks as possible, and using the left arm to balance.

- Hold this position for ten to fifteen seconds, then release.

- Players should swing the right leg forward and backward to continue loosening the muscle they've just stretched before returning to a standing position.

The Left Leg Muscles

- Players should stand straight with their feet apart at shoulder width, arms at their sides.

- Ask players to pull their left legs up behind them with the left arm, bending it at the knee. They should hold the left foot as close to the buttocks as possible, using the right arm to balance.

- Hold this position for ten to fifteen seconds, then release.

- Players should swing the left leg forward and backward to continue loosening the muscle they've just stretched before returning to a standing position.

is no prescribed amount of time to let it heal. It could take a week or it could take months depending on the severity of the pull. Recovering from such an injury can be arduous and painful for young players, especially since their local Little League probably doesn't have the same amenities or facilities that professional teams have when it comes to treating such injuries.

There isn't much a young player can do other than rest and wait when such an injury occurs, and that could cost him an entire season. So remember that the best thing to do before undertaking any serious running or sprinting is to have players stretch the legs properly and often. Ten minutes of stretching a day can prevent a season's worth of injuries.

Leg Bends

- Players should lie on their backs and extend their right legs straight up.

- Ask players to slowly bend the leg at the knee and, using both hands, pull the leg back into the stomach and hold the position for ten to fifteen seconds, then release.

- Players should extend the right leg out and flex it for a few seconds.

- Ask players to extend the left leg straight out while lying on their backs. Pull the leg back into the stomach and repeat the process.

The Hamstring Stretch

- Ask half of the players to lie on their backs, extending their right legs straight up.

- Each player has a partner, who slowly and carefully pushes the player's leg back toward his head, keeping the leg as straight as possible.

- The partners continue to push the leg slowly until the player begins to feel discomfort in the hamstring. Hold the position for ten to fifteen seconds, then stop, release, and flex.

- Repeat the process with the left leg.

JOGGING, SPRINTING, & HOPPING
These seemingly simple procedures are an excellent way to follow up preliminary stretching exercises

So now your players' legs are stretched and they are ready for some action. It's a nice thought, but not so fast. Though your players have stretched their legs and they are seemingly more limber than when they walked onto the field, they aren't ready to be doing any dashes down to first base just yet.

The body, even at a young age, must be ready for the physical exertion that baseball requires. This means going through a whole series of stretches, sprints, and throwing exercises. By performing these exercises, children will make their bodies limber and cut down on the chance of sustaining an injury once they begin playing.

To that end, it is now time to do a little light running. Have

Jogging

- After the preliminary stretching is done, the players should jog around the warning track once or twice to warm up the rest of the body and get better blood flow to the muscles.

- Players should not run at full speed. This exercise is not designed to be a race.

- Rather it is simply used to get a player limber and work up a sweat.

- Have the players walk another lap around the warning track after jogging to cool the body down.

Sprints

- Now sprinting can begin. Line the players up on the foul lines on either side of the field.

- Mark off designated points in the outfield and have the players do sprints of 10, 20, and 30 yards.

- Have the players do three sets of three for each distance, taking a few seconds in between each set to allow them to catch their breath.

- Hydration is key. Players should drink plenty of water during and after the sprint portion of the warm-up.

your team take a few laps at a leisurely pace around the field. Players should move around a little and shake those arms and legs, stretching them just a bit more. Your players can never be too prepared. It only takes an instant to sustain an injury, so an extra few minutes of preparation time is strongly suggested.

Just when you think you have stretched or prepared your team enough, take an extra minute and do some more. It can't be stressed enough how important the legs are to a baseball player's success, and proper care must be taken to prevent injury.

The Hop

- Have the players stand in rows of five in a stationary position.

- Have the players then begin to skip, alternately bringing their knees up to their chests as they advance forward.

- As the players are skipping, have them swing the arm opposite to the leg they have raised over that leg. Repeat that motion with the other arm and leg so that the arms are constantly moving.

- Have them move from one designated point to another in this fashion in sets of three.

The Twist

- Return the players to the stationary position and have them stand with their legs apart to shoulder width.

- Have them begin to move laterally, crossing one leg over the other while rotating the upper body and swinging the arms.

- Have them perform this exercise from one designated point to another and back again in sets of three.

- Remember to have players drink more water and keep hydrated after every step of the exercise process.

PREPARATION

WARMING UP THE ARM
Whether it's a cannon or a popgun, it won't fire if not properly prepared

Far too many arm injuries occur at almost every level from lack of preparation. The notion that you can just step out onto the field, pick up a baseball, and begin firing rockets in every direction is a dangerous one.

That is why it is important to warm the arm up properly. Shoulder and elbow injuries can be devastating; they can not only end seasons, they can also end careers. More and more teenagers these days are undergoing surgeries to repair damage, damage that could have, in most cases, been avoided had the proper care been taken to get the arm ready to throw.

If you see your players throwing too hard too quickly, put a

The Soft Toss

- Have the players stand at close distance to their respective partners. Fifteen or 20 feet is perfect depending on their age and skill level.

- Players should be throwing at 40 percent capacity at this point.

- Remember to stress that there is *no need to push* at this point. The players should not be throwing at 100 percent strength. This is a drill designed to warm the muscles in the arm, shoulder, and elbow.

Extending

- It is time to extend the distance between partners. Have them take a few steps back and double the distance between them.

- Have them increase the strength with which they are throwing but be quick to point out that they should still not be throw-ing at 100 percent capacity, especially if it's still early in the season.

- By now the players should be warm enough to remove any outerwear or jackets that could encumber their throwing motion.

stop to it. Remind them of the dangers of pushing too hard, too quickly. It's a common problem experienced by many professionals each year in spring training. They push too hard too soon and suffer injuries, all because they are eager to get out on the field and play.

Remember that you are the coach and your word is law. Don't ask; tell them that they will follow your throwing program. Otherwise, they can take a seat.

The Next Step

- Have the players move to a distance of about 100 feet apart.

- They can begin throwing harder, almost at maximum effort. But remind them that they still are not at a point where they can push themselves.

- This is especially true of pitchers, whose arms need even more special care than those of the position players.

- Be sure that all the players use the proper throwing motion and avoid sidearm and slingshot tactics.

YELLOW 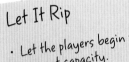 LIGHT

The spring is when many injuries occur, particularly in colder climates. Be sure that before having your players head out of the clubhouse, they are wearing the proper clothing. Always wear layers, especially on the upper half of the body. As players get warmer, have them take off the layers. Be sure that once they stop playing, the players put the outerwear back on to prevent the muscles from tightening.

Let It Rip

- Let the players begin throwing at 100 percent capacity.

- Monitor them closely, though. Do not allow them to show off their arms by throwing great distances or by trying to reach a certain figure on the radar gun.

- Though the arms are now loose enough to be throwing at 100 percent, it is not advisable to take foolish chances. Players can be severely injured by trying to do too much with their arms.

PREPARATION

TELL THE COACH WHEN IT HURTS
Make sure your players follow this simple rule

No one likes getting hurt. But if you are going to play a sport, whether it is baseball or bocci, basketball or badminton, injuries are bound to occur. Someone will step the wrong way or twist a way she shouldn't be twisting and the inevitable muscle pull will come into play.

It is what someone does after she gets hurt that can make all the difference in preventing further injury. You are the adult in the situation so you must take charge. Stress early

and often to your players that hiding an injury will not be tolerated. No good can come out of not telling an adult that an injury has occurred.

Let the children know that they will not lose their place on the team just because they have suffered an injury. If a player has to sit out a practice or a game because she is hurt, explain to her that it is smarter for her to rest and get healthy rather than risk further injury. If the child gets upset or doesn't agree

Pay Attention during Warm-ups

- Keep an eye on your players during warm-ups. Watch for players clutching at their shoulders, elbows, or hamstrings. Be aware if any players are doubling over. It is a sign that something could be wrong.

- Stress that at the first hint of discomfort, they should

inform one of the coaches immediately.

- There is no way of predicting when an injury will occur. Encourage the players to monitor themselves and understand their bodies better in an effort to prevent some injuries.

Stopping

- Tell your players to *stop* whatever they are doing, whether it is running, throwing, hitting, or stretching, if they feel they are injured or are experiencing any discomfort. Continuing to play under these circumstances is dangerous and can lead to a more severe injury.

- Believe your players when they tell you they are hurt. You are asking them to get to know their bodies and their limitations, so you must trust them when they tell you something doesn't feel right.

with you, then it is time to bring in the parent. Occasionally a parent may side with the child, but you should have the final say on whether or not you believe a player is healthy enough to be on the field.

As a coach, you must also respect a player when she tells you she is hurt. Believe them and do not play them when they are not 100 percent. If you have any concerns or questions about the child's health, consult the parent. Ultimately, the decision to pull a child from a game or practice resides with the parent anyway, so make sure the person who is responsible for that child's well-being is informed immediately of any injury.

Finding an Adult

- Under ideal circumstances, you would be able to see everyone and everything that is going on during a practice or game.

- Because you can't, stress that if a player gets injured or feels sick he should find a coach or parent immediately and let him know what the problem is.

- Instruct your players to explain in great detail what hurts, what they were doing when they suffered the injury, and whether they need to involve a parent.

Honesty

- There is no shame in getting hurt. Lying about it or attempting to hide it, however, is another matter.

- Pay particular attention to your older players who have more invested in the game. They are more likely to conceal an injury in order to stay on the field.

- Stress to your older players that if they suffer an injury or believe they have suffered an injury, they must be honest and come forward.

- Tell players that if they suspect one of their teammates has suffered or is hiding an injury, they should encourage him to come forward.

COMMON INJURIES
Knowing what the common injuries are can help in their prevention

Chances are that most coaches aren't doctors, registered nurses, or health care professionals. That, however, should not preclude a coach from familiarizing himself with the most common sports injuries and how they should be initially treated. As a coach, you are not required to perform any sort of medical procedure. But understanding the signs and symptoms of an injury, whether big or small, will instill greater confidence in your players and their parents.

Keep a well-stocked medical kit with you at all times, one that includes bandages, disinfectants, cold sprays, wraps for sprained ankles, gauze, etc. Do not, however, administer any medication. Also, be sure that you have a list of any player allergies as well as the proper course of action should they experience an attack.

Some Little League fields also have defibrillators handy. Take a course on how to use it. A first aid class or CPR course

The Hamstring

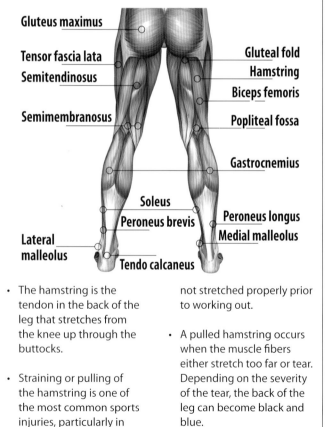

- The hamstring is the tendon in the back of the leg that stretches from the knee up through the buttocks.

- Straining or pulling of the hamstring is one of the most common sports injuries, particularly in baseball, and can occur if not stretched properly prior to working out.

- A pulled hamstring occurs when the muscle fibers either stretch too far or tear. Depending on the severity of the tear, the back of the leg can become black and blue.

The Quadriceps

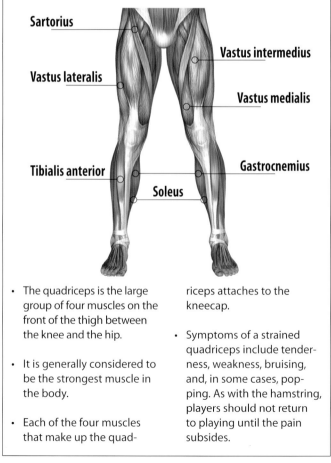

- The quadriceps is the large group of four muscles on the front of the thigh between the knee and the hip.

- It is generally considered to be the strongest muscle in the body.

- Each of the four muscles that make up the quadriceps attaches to the kneecap.

- Symptoms of a strained quadriceps include tenderness, weakness, bruising, and, in some cases, popping. As with the hamstring, players should not return to playing until the pain subsides.

is also a good idea if you are going to be responsible for the health and well-being of your team. If you are prepared for any emergency, from a broken leg to a broken fingernail, it will make all the difference when caring for your players.

The Groin

- The groin is composed of three muscles located on the inside of the thigh.

- While stretching too much or stress can cause a groin muscle pull, excessive contact can also cause a pull.

- Symptoms of a groin pull include lack of strength in the adductor muscles, stiffness, bruising, and pain.

- A groin can take up to three months to heal depending on the severity of the pull.

The Elbow

- Some elbow discomfort or inflammation is common when throwing for the first time in months.

- Players should apply ice to the affected area as quickly as possible after throwing and stop throwing if pain persists. If pain continues or increases, see a doctor.

- Little League elbow can occur in young pitchers who throw too much before puberty. The ligament on the inside of the elbow begins to pull away from the bone.

- According to some top experts, this can be avoided by not throwing curveballs and sliders.

PREPARATION

STRETCHING WITH THE BAT
A bat is an excellent tool for limbering up prior to a game or practice

So you think that a bat is used only for hitting. Well, guess again. If you want to get limber, then grab the lumber.

Using the bat to stretch and get loose is an excellent complement to the techniques and exercises that were discussed earlier in this chapter. As a coach, you will find that baseball is a great deal like other sports in that the better players always seem to have the tools of their trade at hand. Basketball players are continually holding or dribbling a ball; golfers spend

lots of hours off the course simply holding or swinging a club; and football players can always be found tossing a ball in the air, even if it's only to themselves.

Getting the feel for your equipment is part of the game, and by using the bat as part of the training regimen players can get a better feel for the lumber (or aluminum). What would they be doing with the bat if they weren't stretching with it anyway? Leaning on it? Swinging it idly? Of course they

Behind the Back

- Have the players stand with legs spread shoulder width apart, holding the bat behind them at the waist with the arms hooked around the lumber.

- While holding the bat, players swivel the upper half of the body left and right as

far as possible without it causing any discomfort to stretch the back muscles.

- Each stretch should be held at its farthest point for several seconds before releasing. Perform this exercise in sets of three.

Bat above the Head

- Have the players stand with legs spread shoulder width apart while holding the bat above their heads. Their hands should be at opposite ends of the bat and not in the middle.

- Have the players bend over at the waist and touch their

toes with the bat. Hold the position for five seconds and repeat in sets of three.

- Return to the original position with the bat over the head and perform squats in sets of three, holding each squat for five seconds.

would. It's natural—as natural as using it to stretch.

While a bat works to perform these types of exercises, any pole, piece of lumber, or metal tubing will do. Generally these exercises shouldn't be performed indoors or in close quarters for safety reasons.

·················· RED ● LIGHT ··············

While using a bat to warm up is a good idea, one must do so carefully. Swinging a bat or flipping it around carelessly without checking to see if anyone is standing nearby can result in serious injury. Teach players to check the immediate area and never swing a bat in the dugout.

Bat behind the Head

- Have the players stand with legs spread shoulder width apart while holding the bat behind their heads, resting it across the neck. Their hands should be at opposite ends of the bat and not in the middle.

- Have the players, while holding onto the bat, swivel their upper torsos from side to side, holding each stretch at its farthest point for five seconds before releasing. Perform this exercise in sets of three.

The Weighted Bat

- Have the players take a weighted bat, either one that has a doughnut or is weighted naturally, and swing it back and forth at a moderate speed.

- Tell the players to swing the bat with either arm in long, looping circles in a sideways helicopter fashion.

- Remember to use caution when performing these and any other drills that involve a bat. Be sure there is a safe enough distance between the player holding the bat and her teammates.

PREPARATION

47

PATIENCE

The younger the child, the more patience is required

The joy of watching a five-year-old play baseball for the first time is matched only by the frustration that can ensue when said five-year-old has his attention drawn away by a butterfly, the dirt, the wind, the color of his hat, or the fact that his mom is sitting in the stands with his baby brother.

It sounds all so stereotypical, like something out of a bad romantic comedy. The bottom line, however, is that it is true—all of it. This is the most difficult age to coach simply because the attention span isn't there and neither, in most cases, is the physical ability. Most children this age are excited about the prospects of playing baseball as a result of an enthusiastic parent.

Don't misunderstand, though. There are some children this age that actually love baseball, can follow the game, and perform admirably on the field without any encouragement from their parents.

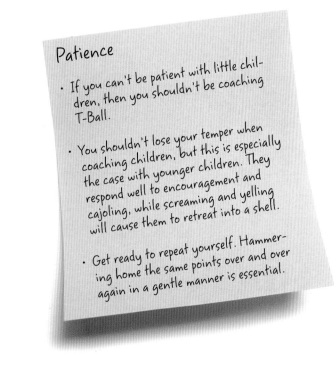

Patience

- If you can't be patient with little children, then you shouldn't be coaching T-Ball.

- You shouldn't lose your temper when coaching children, but this is especially the case with younger children. They respond well to encouragement and cajoling, while screaming and yelling will cause them to retreat into a shell.

- Get ready to repeat yourself. Hammering home the same points over and over again in a gentle manner is essential.

Lack of Focus

- Younger children—ages five and six—often cannot stay focused on the task at hand for more than a few moments.

- Try to have at least two assistant coaches. Have one of them provide one-on-one instruction while you work with the rest of the team. The children will respond better to the individual attention and show more of the focus they lack in a larger group setting.

But for the most part, prepare yourself for an arduous season. It means being patient. Very, very patient. It means repeating yourself over and over and over again until you can give the same speech in your sleep. It means understanding that not every player is the coach's son or daughter and that extra time and special care has to be taken in order for every child's needs to be met.

While it all seems like a daunting task—and it is—the rewards are beautiful. Watching the youngsters grow and learn over the course of the season brings a feeling that won't be matched too often in your coaching career. The first big catch, the first big hit, and the first near-perfect throw will elicit screams and howls from the players, your staff, and the parents, making all the hard work that went into the season worth it.

Talking to the Kids

- A coach should never, ever yell at the children.

- There is nothing a child can do that will warrant your losing your patience to a point that you need to scream or raise your voice.

- Speak calmly and carefully. Children are literal. Mean what you say, and avoid figures of speech. Children will not understand them, and it will only make your job more difficult.

- Encourage the children to ask questions.

Expectations

- Don't set the bar too high.

- Remember that children this age have likely never picked up a glove, ball, or bat prior to meeting you. Assuming they know how to use the aforementioned pieces of equipment would be a mistake.

- Expect to be frustrated. Mistakes, miscues, and general mayhem usually accompany a T-Ball game or practice, so be ready for it.

- But expect to laugh too. Children this age are usually as cute and funny as any you will encounter.

THE TEE
That big hunk of rubber or plastic can be an intimidator or a friend

The first time a child picks up a baseball bat and approaches the tee is a highlight in her young life. Chances are this is the day Mom or Dad has been dreaming of for years, and there will likely be a great deal of pressure on the youngster to perform. It is your job to release that pressure valve.

The tee can be very intimidating. Children see the ball sitting atop it and can become apprehensive. It is your job to keep them calm and walk them through these critical moments.

You do not want the children becoming down or depressed about coming to the plate. Encourage them energetically and often, regardless of how they do.

That said, there will always be one or two children on your team who will step up to the tee, get in a perfect stance, and line a shot over second base. Applaud them and encourage them as well. But also know where to draw the line. Don't let them show off too much. It can be embarrassing for the

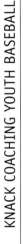

The Tee

- Most of the tees used are adjustable in height with a sliding column inside another tube and are attached to a base shaped like home plate. There is a cup, or holder, atop the inner tube on which the baseball rests.

- Tees are generally made of durable rubber or plastic.

- The rubber tees tend to have a larger shelf life because they are more flexible and last longer despite being pounded constantly with the bat.

Whom Does It Help

- Most children ages four through six have trouble swinging the bat and cannot hit a pitched ball.

- The tee allows them to swing at a stationary target and make contact.

- Because the tee is adjustable, children of all heights and sizes can take advantage of its benefits.

- Older players, even adults, use the tee as well, as a practice tool to work on their swings.

other children, who will often compare their abilities with those of their teammates.

This is a very critical time in your season. Some children are shy and awkward and some need to be drawn out slowly. Pay particular attention to them and remember to stay patient.

ZOOM

So who are you going to believe? The towns of Albion, Michigan, and Starkville, Mississippi, have each laid claim to being the birthplace of T-Ball. No one knows for sure but one thing is known—T-Ball has been around for at least a half century with millions of kids playing, including at the White House.

No Shame

- Some players can get embarrassed because they have trouble hitting a pitched ball. Others even have trouble using the tee itself, hitting the column more than they hit the baseball.

- Stress to your players that there is no shame in using the tee. It is a learning tool and all part of the process of becoming a better ballplayer.

- Take your time with these players and be gentle but firm with them.

Don't Pitch

- Some of the players may actually be accomplished enough to swing at live pitching. Don't give in to the temptation.

- Pitching to some players and using the tee with others will only lead to animosity and hurt feelings. This is T-Ball. All the players should use the tee.

- If a player knows how to hit, keep her after practice and work privately with her or have the parent do it.

T-BALL

51

THE BAT
Using the bat can be fun, but be careful when and where you swing it

Have you ever watched batting practice at a high school, college, or professional game? Hitting is fun. There usually isn't a player, even pitchers, who don't like to step into the batter's box and take a few hacks. The same can said all the way down to T-Ball.

The children love to swing the bat; very often they'll swing it wherever they are standing. Now that you have gotten them past the tee and have helped them understand its purpose, let's start working on the bat. Lay some ground rules for bats and batting right from the outset. That way you will avoid problems later on.

For starters, don't allow any of the "But that's my bat" cries that

Bigger Isn't Better

- The bat should not be less than 24 inches or more than 27 inches. It should also not be larger than 2¼ inches in diameter.

- Do not be tempted to use "gimmick" bats with larger barrels, or bats for toddlers that have enormous, cartoon-like barrels.

- The premise is simple—get the children comfortable swinging a regular bat. The sooner they learn how to swing one the easier the game will become.

Choking Up

- There is no reason for a five-year-old to be gripping a bat at the knob and swinging for the fences. Always have them choke up.

- Squash the "grip it and rip it" philosophy right from the outset. Teach bat control early on and let a player's natural abil-

ity determine down the line whether or not he is capable of swinging without choking up.

- Explain that choking up on the bat will produce more hits.

can originate from youngsters who see a teammate grab their bat and head to the plate. Explain that they are part of a team and as such, there is a certain amount of sharing that goes on and that includes allowing a teammate to use your bat.

Remember, too, to remind them to be careful when they are swinging. A serious injury can occur if they swing a bat without looking first. Designate an area other than the plate in which players can swing the bat to warm up. No one but the person carrying the bat is allowed in that area. Remember to have your players wear a helmet around the on-deck circle.

Aluminum

- Most of the bats players will use at this age are made from aluminum. They are durable and can handle the rigors of being owned by a small child.

- Aluminum bats are often lighter, easier to swing, and, when used properly,

produce more dramatic results.

- Some parents will buy their children wooden bats. Don't dissuade this practice. Whatever makes the youngster comfortable is what you should encourage.

No Bat Throwing

- Throwing a bat after a player has hit the ball is not allowed.

- Stress this point in as loud a manner as is acceptable. Players and coaches can get hurt if a youngster throws a bat after swinging it.

- Teach them early in the hitting process to drop the bat before running to first base. If this is drilled into a player early, he likely won't start throwing the bat when he gets older.

T-BALL

53

THE SWING

Establishing a solid swing pattern early will help avoid problems later

More than catching, more than throwing, swinging the bat is the act that children cherish the most when it comes to baseball. The cries of "I hit first, I hit first" resonate from diamonds across the country and with good reason. The feeling of the ball and bat coming together to produce a hit provides the batter with one of the best feelings imaginable.

But before you can even begin to think about connecting for that hit, you need to work on the swing. Sure, at this age, the swing is not going to be a masterpiece. Regardless of how light the bat is or how well you believe that you have prepared your player to step up to the tee, inevitably the swing turns into a mess.

What Side, Coach?

- Establish immediately whether the player hits right-handed or left-handed.

- The same basic principles apply to hitting from either side, but if you have a left-handed hitting coach to demonstrate technique it would make instructing the younger left-handed children a bit easier.

- Do not attempt to create switch hitters at this age. Worry about teaching your players to hit from their natural side of the plate. They will have time to move to the opposite side of the plate as they get older.

Do It Right

- If you are going to teach them how to hit, don't take shortcuts.

- Teach them the same way you would teach a fifteen-year-old. Use the same terms and the same demonstrations. They may be young, but if they see you do it, they will be able to imitate it.

- Don't let the players be lazy with their swings. Make them swing properly from the outset so bad habits don't develop early.

It's not your fault. It's not the child's fault. It's nature's fault. Most five-year-olds are not coordinated enough to step up to the tee and start swinging with any authority or consistency. It takes practice—lots and lots of practice. So don't be worried if you explain to your players the proper swing techniques and they don't have them mastered in a matter of moments.

The swings will be too fast, too slow, too high, and too low. The players will likely be stepping in the bucket, stepping on their own toes, stepping everywhere but where they should be. That's where you come in. Give them a nice, simple, easy swing pattern. Stress the importance of making contact and reward even the slightest bit of contact between ball and bat with the requisite applause.

That type of encouragement is just as important as the proper technique at this stage. If the child feels as if he's doing well and succeeding, he'll want to continue. If he feels as if he's failed, then you can run the risk of losing him.

The Motion

- Have players crouch, stride, and swing.

- Don't let them stand stiff-legged or straight up. Have them bend slightly at the knees in the proper stance with their chin tucked in and facing the pitcher's mound.

- Have them practice the swinging motion from this position several times before allowing them to jump right up to the tee.

- You must stay patient in order for them to be patient. There should be no swinging at the ball without a few practice swings first.

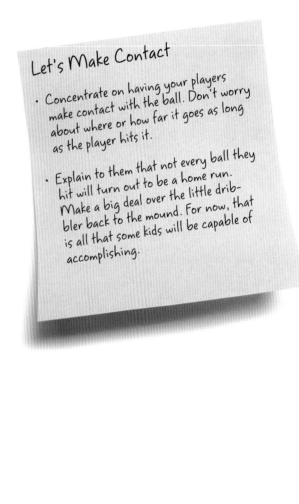

Let's Make Contact

- Concentrate on having your players make contact with the ball. Don't worry about where or how far it goes as long as the player hits it.

- Explain to them that not every ball they hit will turn out to be a home run. Make a big deal over the little dribbler back to the mound. For now, that is all that some kids will be capable of accomplishing.

THROWING & CATCHING

Starting off slowly will make it easier to teach a player how to catch and throw

Be sure that you have plenty of time and patience when you begin working on throwing and catching. These two acts are among the more difficult for most children to master. Even older kids have trouble catching the ball and throwing it consistently, so it would only stand to reason that the youngest age group would certainly have some issues.

Don't worry, though, because there are a few things that you can do to make this experience a bit easier for you and your players. Start by having a little short toss. Have them stand just a few feet from one another and toss the ball to each other underhanded. This will allow them the chance to actually make a catch while giving them the chance to see

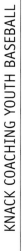

The Basics

- Throwing at this age is often difficult because of coordination problems. Go through the basics and have them imitate you.

- Many children this age have never picked up a baseball before, so don't be discouraged by what you see.

- Tell your players never to throw a ball at someone when that person isn't looking. Explain to them that you could seriously injure someone if you throw a baseball at another person and they don't see it coming.

The Southpaw

- A large percentage of your players could be left-handed.

- In the event you have any left-handed players on your team, try to have a left-handed coach or parent on hand to demonstrate these drills.

- Children are literal. It will be easier for a left-handed player to imitate a left-handed coach rather than watching a right-handed coach throw the ball.

- Once you have determined a player is left-handed, continue to have him throw left-handed.

what it is like to throw a ball, even if it is underhanded.

Go through this drill for a few minutes before having them switch to an overhand throw. Remind them not to throw the ball too hard. Too many children get hit in the face each year with thrown balls because they aren't quick enough or experienced enough to get their gloves up in time to offer protection.

No Fear

- Fear is often the biggest obstacle for youngsters when it comes to catching a ball.

- Explain to them that while it is only natural to be afraid of getting hurt by the ball, that's why they have a glove.

- Have them use two hands when catching the ball.

- Style points need not be awarded. Just catching the ball will be an accomplishment in and of itself for many children this age.

The Body

- Explain to the players that they should use their bodies to catch the ball if necessary.

- Demonstrate how to trap the ball against their body. While this is not an ideal way to catch the ball, it is a perfect drill to get them to hold onto the ball.

- The more they hold onto the ball, either trapping it or catching it, the more their confidence will grow.

T-BALL

FIELDING

Do not push too much when it comes to teaching fielding; slower is better

The first piece of advice for coaches teaching youngsters how to field for the first time is to be careful. Don't get too carried away with hitting grounders, at least not at the start. Chances are that a ground ball heading in their direction will not produce the kind of play for which you are hoping, and harder hit ground balls can result in injuries.

Rather, simply roll the ball to your players. The ball doesn't have to be traveling at a snail's pace, but it shouldn't be going too fast, either. The point is that you are setting the players up to succeed. If the ball is moving slowly enough, they will be able to grab it. At the very least, they will have a chance to knock it down or stop it, and if that occurs, let them know

No Wolf Pack

- The wolf pack approach to fielding is prevalent at this age.

- Breaking this habit is one of the toughest to do simply because children this age are like puppies. They see the ball and they chase it.

- Stress to your team that every player need not go after every ball that is hit. Stay in position and wait for the ball to get hit to you. Everyone will have a chance to make plays.

No Fear

- The ball used in T-Ball is soft and generally is not hit very hard.

- The chances of getting hurt by a batted ball are minimal. If players are afraid they will get hurt, they will never field the ball.

- Prepare them for getting hit with the ball. Demonstrate that even if they do get hit with it, there will be more discomfort than pain and that it is easily shaken off.

they have done something well.

Be sure when rolling the ball to the player that initially you are rolling the ball directly at them. The idea of having to move laterally to field a grounder is one that they haven't grasped yet. Warm them up slowly from a few feet away so they can see the ball coming and still have enough time to prepare to field it.

The Basics

- Go through the basics of fielding a ground ball.

- There is no need to get in-depth here. A quick overview of how to stand in the ready position, how to prepare if a ball comes toward you, and how to knock it down will suffice.

- The objective is to have them keep the ball in front of them. Remind them to not throw their glove, hat, shoes, teammates, etc., at the ball in an attempt to stop it.

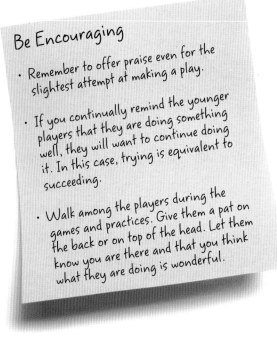

Be Encouraging

- Remember to offer praise even for the slightest attempt at making a play.

- If you continually remind the younger players that they are doing something well, they will want to continue doing it. In this case, trying is equivalent to succeeding.

- Walk among the players during the games and practices. Give them a pat on the back or on top of the head. Let them know you are there and that you think what they are doing is wonderful.

T-BALL

59

GETTING STARTED
The proper approach to an at-bat will lead to a successful plate appearance

Getting your players prepared for their plate appearances is as important as the plate appearances themselves. The best way to prepare is to develop a routine and get into a rhythm. Have your players repeat what they do before every at-bat over and over again, especially if they have been having success at the plate. They'll want to repeat their pre–at-bat ritual if they see they are doing well.

If you have them follow that simple routine, what they do before they step up to the plate and what they do once they are in the batter's box becomes second nature. You do not want your players thinking too much heading into an at-bat. This can lead to nervousness and thinking too much at the

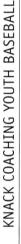

The Proper Bat

- Finding the right size bat isn't only important in T-Ball, it is important at every level to maintain a well-balanced swing.

- If the bat is too long or too heavy, it will drag through the strike zone and every swing will be late, likely producing a grounder or a popup to the opposite field.

- If the bat is too small or too light, the swing will be too quick and the batter will be out in front of every pitch.

Warm-up

- Encourage players to watch the opposing pitcher from the on-deck circle to get a sense of how hard he is throwing and what his location is like.

- Players should take a few swings as the opposing pitcher is throwing to the current batter to get a sense of timing with his pitches.

- Have your players take a few more practice swings before they step into the batter's box to ensure they are loose.

plate. You should be doing the thinking for them at this point. Keep the decision-making process to a minimum where they are concerned.

Hitting is complicated enough even for accomplished players. Younger players have enough to worry about just making contact during an at-bat. Therefore it would behoove you to have them get into a simple but consistent pattern before and during every at-bat.

Keeping it simple is the best approach. Tell your players that all they need to do is grab a bat, take a few proper swings—the key word there being proper—and go hit the ball. Don't complicate matters by trying to have them do too much.

Show confidence in them, as well. A pat on the back or a strong word of encouragement as they head to the plate or onto the on-deck circle can make all the difference with some children. If you are confident in them, they will be confident in themselves. If they have that confidence, they will be sure of their pre–plate appearance routine and it should make the at-bat a more comfortable, stress-free situation.

Get Comfortable

- Players should not be afraid to do a little "housekeeping" when they step into the batter's box, smoothing out the dirt to their liking and filling in any holes left by previous batters.

- Tell players to treat each at-bat as the most important at-bat of the day. That means making sure the conditions are as ideal as possible.

- Block out distractions such as the fans, parents, friends, and teammates. Focus on the task at hand.

Get Rhythm

- Good hitters usually have good rhythm. Have players maintain their rhythm while in the batter's box.

- Discourage players from stepping out of the batter's box after every pitch, adjusting their batting gloves and helmets, or taking a time-out.

- Explain that being ready to hit puts the onus on the pitcher to keep the game moving along. Staying in the batter's box and being prepared can take the pitcher out of *his* rhythm.

THE STANCE

Every player's batting stance is different, though the basic principles remain the same

Whether a player stands with his legs ridiculously far apart at the plate or too close together is a matter of taste and comfort. Whether he holds his hands high or low, near his body or away, is also a matter of personal preference. Ultimately, if a player is going to succeed at the plate, he has to feel comfortable.

Your job as coach, however, is to teach your players the basics and make sure that they stick as closely to those points as possible. As players get older, the rules are open for interpretation and they can employ whatever style points they wish as long as they continue to hit. But when players are younger, it is important that they first learn the proper stance

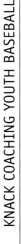
Setting Up

- Have your player stand at the plate with his feet spread shoulder-length apart and with his toes turned in slightly.

- He should not be flat-footed. Rather he should be leaning forward just a bit and ready to move.

- Being flat-footed or leaning back on the heels will produce an unbalanced swing.

- Be careful he is not leaning forward too far. This will also produce an unbalanced, unreliable swing.

The Width

- Ideally, the players should have their feet line up with the front edge of the plate and the back edge of the plate where the square portion ends.

- If the player's legs are too far apart, he will be off balance and unable to stride into the ball properly when he swings.

- If the player's alignment is not parallel to the plate, then the pitcher can gain an advantage by pitching to either the inside or outside corner.

and the proper techniques regarding hitting before they begin implementing their own variations.

While some children attempt to imitate what they see their favorite players do on television, it is your job to remind them that the players they are watching are professionals. They have been playing baseball and hitting for a long time and as a result, know what works best for them. Point out to them that the players on television had to learn how to hit at some point as well and that they followed the basic rules when they were starting out.

Ultimately you do not want to have a group of robots that all look alike when they step to the plate. You are the knowledgeable one, though. Give them the basics of the stance and drill them constantly until what you have taught becomes second nature. Once they have demonstrated that they have an understanding of how to stand at the plate and approach an at-bat properly, then you can loosen the reins and let them begin to experiment.

Bend Those Knees

- Instruct your players to keep their knees slightly bent when they set up.

- This will help provide the necessary balance at the plate and shrink the strike zone a bit.

- If the player's legs are straight, it will impact his stride and make swinging the bat more difficult.

- The bent knees put the batter in a position to be able to react to the pitch quicker and more fluidly.

The Elbow Myth

- Have the batter set up with his top hand just about even with his shoulder.

- Having the batter set up with their "elbow up," a popular instruction among coaches, actually creates a bad swing.

- When the batter has the elbow up too high, it must come down during the swing. Often it comes down too far and the batter ends up swinging in an upward arc, thus popping the ball up.

THE GRIP
Knowing how to hold the bat properly is the first step toward becoming a good hitter

Every at-bat should be treated as its own entity. It has a life of its own with a beginning, middle, and end that is unique to that plate appearance. What should not be special about the at-bat is the way the player holds the bat. That should be a constant from one at-bat to the next.

One of the first things that a coach needs to teach a hitter is how to hold the bat properly. If a player does not have a proper grip or does not understand the concepts surrounding the grip, then the at-bat is in jeopardy before it ever has a chance to take place.

When the proper grip is executed, the player's hands will be stacked one on top of another when holding the bat. If there

Holding the Bat

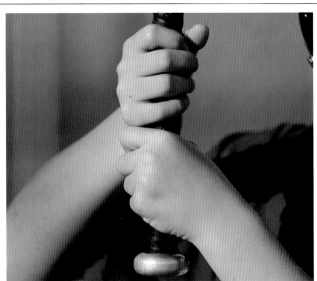

- The bat should be held in the fingers just below where they join the hand and not in the palms of the hand.

- Holding the bat in this fashion affords the hitter more flexibility and promotes better swing control.

- Young hitters should not experiment with more complicated grips until they have mastered the proper basic grip.

- Holding the bat at more of an angle is recommended. Holding the bat parallel to the body will produce a bit of an uppercut in the swing.

The Knuckles

- The middle knuckles on each hand should line up if the bat is being held properly.

- If the knuckles on the bottom hand wrap too much around the barrel and don't line up with those of the top hand, bat speed will suffer.

- By opening and closing the knuckles, however, the batter can have a better chance of hitting the ball to left and right field, respectively.

is a gap between their hands, then it will be more difficult to swing the bat. This applies whether the player is choking up on the bat or holding it down on the knob. You should not be able to see any wood or metal between the hands when the player is holding the bat. The only time the player's hands should be apart on the bat is when bunting.

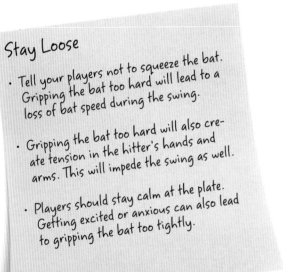

Stay Loose

- Tell your players not to squeeze the bat. Gripping the bat too hard will lead to a loss of bat speed during the swing.

- Gripping the bat too hard will also create tension in the hitter's hands and arms. This will impede the swing as well.

- Players should stay calm at the plate. Getting excited or anxious can also lead to gripping the bat too tightly.

Choking Up

- Gripping the bat a few inches above the knob is called choking up.

- Choking up allows a hitter to have greater bat control and makes it easier for the hitter to shorten her swing when necessary.

- Encourage your younger players to choke up. Most young players are not strong enough to swing without choking up.

- Holding the bat at the knob and "swinging for the fences" at an early age will create bad hitting habits.

THE STRIDE

Learning about stepping into a pitch can be a confusing process for younger hitters

Teaching young hitters about striding into a pitch during the swing can often be a difficult concept for them to grasp. How many times have you seen a young player take a definitive step toward the mound before the pitch is even thrown and then swing flat-footed when the ball arrives? How about swinging without striding at all?

It happens more often than you would think simply because younger players do not understand. The best way to help them to understand is to preach patience. They need to keep their hands back and cocked as long as possible before swinging. Have them keep their weight shifted onto the back foot as long as possible as well.

Do Not Lunge

- It is very important that the hitter stride into the pitch. Lunging will dramatically change the swing, taking away bat control and power.

- Lunging also diminishes bat speed.

- Have the batter draw a line in the dirt in the front of the batter's box, about 12 inches from where his front foot is when taking the stance. If the batter can keep his foot from crossing the line, he will not lunge or overstride.

Going Forward

- The hitter's front foot should move toward the pitcher.

- Too often young hitters "bail out" or "step in the bucket." This is the act of opening up as they swing and stepping to the right or left instead of forward as they swing.

- If the batter "bails out," he cannot see the pitch properly and therefore has little chance of hitting the ball.

- The stride should be short and not exaggerated, less than a foot in length.

By doing this, it will make for a quicker, more effective swing. To help promote patience, have the hitter turn the front hip and shoulder slightly inward as the pitcher goes into the windup. This act, though seemingly insignificant, will provide the split second needed to ensure a proper swing as the ball is arriving at the plate.

Remember to stress that the hitter must stride forward when beginning the swing. It is important to step into the ball and make contact while going forward.

MAKE IT EASY

Place a 2X6, cinder blocks, or any other object that can be lined up behind the batter. Have the batter stride forward using the lumber or the blocks as a guide for practice. Do not let him step over the wood or blocks. This is an effective practice method that will keep a hitter's stride true.

Pointing the Foot

- The hitter should have her front foot pointed at a bit of an angle toward home plate, with her heel up and her toes pointing downward.

- This position will provide better balance for the hitter and, ideally, make it more difficult for her to "bail out" on a pitch.

- The hitter should come down on the inside of the front foot when striding as the swing begins.

Be Patient

- This is probably the toughest part of the stride to master.

- If players are too eager, they will begin their swing too early and start the stride too early. Stress to your players to wait on the pitch before beginning their stride.

- The hitter shouldn't rush the stride because that will rush the movement of the hands and change the entire tempo of the at-bat.

SWINGING

Getting into the swing of an at-bat can be a fun learning process

The swing itself is one of the most exciting moments in a baseball game. Have you ever been to a big game or watched one on television and seen all the flashbulbs going off as the batter begins his swing? People want to see it because anything can happen on any given swing: a home run, a line drive, or even a dribbler. The results of a swing are unpredictable.

What should be predictable, though, is the physical act of swinging. It's an action that once learned should be repeated the same way over and over again. Naturally there will be slight variations from time to time as a hitter makes adjustments depending on the pitcher or the game situation, but the basic principles of the swing should always be the same.

When dealing with younger players, do not let them freelance or try out different methods, at least not during a game or in practice. If they want to experiment on their own, that's one thing, but if they are under your watchful eye then teach

Watch the Ball

- Finding the ball's release point is essential to picking up its flight to the plate.

- Watching the ball as the pitcher completes his delivery and releases it will enable the hitter to determine the movement of the pitch and whether it is an off-speed pitch or a fastball.

- Encourage players to keep an eye on the ball through the point of contact.

The Pivot

- As the hitter begins her swing, the back leg should begin to bend and curl inward toward the pitcher.

- The back foot will come off the ground and begin to pivot but should never break contact with the ground.

- The back knee should begin to turn and the foot will roll over, completing the pivot.

them the proper basics of the swing and have them stick to it until they can perform the act without thinking.

Exploding Hips

- The hips provide much of the power in the swing.

- The hitter should begin to thrust her hips as she begins her swing. The hips will start to rotate toward the ball as the hitter swings and will eventually wind up facing the pitcher when the swing is completed properly.

- The hitter should use the hips as a guide in the swing. If turned properly, the rest of the body will follow and the swing has a better chance of being correct.

The Follow-through

- The hitter's wrists have broken and rolled as he finishes the swing. Depending on the hitter's style, the bat should now be on or next to the front shoulder.

- The shoulder that was in the back as the swing began is now forward after the body has rotated.

- The hitter's chin should be down on the rear shoulder with the eyes locked on the point of contact.

- The back foot should have pivoted onto the ball of the foot but should not have broken contact with the ground.

CONCEPTS FOR OLDER PLAYERS

Players who are more advanced can improve their skills by practicing different hitting techniques

As your players get older and more involved with the game, it will be easier to discuss and practice more complicated concepts in regard to hitting. Hitting is an art form. To some, it's a religion. Ted Williams was one of the most brilliant hitters ever to play the game because he immersed himself in the art of hitting and remained a student of the practice his entire life.

No one is predicting that any of your charges will become the next Ted Williams simply because they work hard and understand difficult concepts. One of the keys to becoming a better hitter, especially as one gets older, is to put oneself in a position to become a better hitter.

That means thinking about hitting, visualizing what can be

The Off-speed Pitch

- Batters need to be able to recognize the pitch when it comes out of the pitcher's hand. Pitch recognition usually comes with time and experience.

- A batter should wait on the offering as long as possible once they have determined it is an off-speed pitch.

- Tell players they should learn to think like a pitcher, understanding when it is an appropriate time in the count to throw an off-speed pitch.

- Being able to anticipate when an off-speed pitch will be thrown will make it easier to hit the pitch.

The Opposite Field

- Stress to your players that attempting to pull an outside pitch will usually have disappointing results, i.e., a popup or a weak grounder.

- Show players how to adjust the grip if they are looking to go the other way by turning the bottom hand more toward the field to which they are attempting to hit the ball.

- Encourage players to wait on the pitch as long as possible. The hitter has a better chance of going the other way with a pitch if he is patient.

done with a bat in hand. Have your older players approach their practice sessions and at-bats with vision. Talk to them about hitting in certain situations. An at-bat shouldn't be just stepping to the plate and trying to hit a home run.

Tell your players to pay attention to how the pitcher has worked previous batters in a game and use that information when they get to the plate. If they are serious about hitting, they will study every little nuance and use it to their advantage.

MAKE IT EASY

A batting tee isn't only for T-Ball. Those wanting to get in extra work on their swing have used this simple piece of equipment for generations. Hitters can practice by themselves, moving the tee around to simulate outside pitches and inside pitches when a coach or another player aren't available to throw batting practice.

Practice

- Teach players proper hitting techniques, then practice them over and over again until they become second nature.

- Make sure players go to the batting cage as often as possible.

- Stress the importance of batting practice, particularly against left-handers or a coach throwing only off-speed pitches. It will help the hitter recognize those pitches in game situations.

- Use the batting tee and the soft-toss as tools to improve the swing.

Confidence
- The mental aspect of hitting is just as important as the physical aspects. Being confident in one's abilities can go a long way in turning an average hitter into a good one.

- Don't let one or two bad games impact a player's approach at the plate. Everyone has bad stretches and bad games. Remember that even the best hitters only get a hit three out of every ten at-bats.

71

THE GRIP

Learning how to hold a bat during a bunt is not complicated

It is a shame watching some Major Leaguers these days when they attempt to bunt. Many of them do not have much of an idea about how to lay down a bunt, let alone how to hold the bat while doing so. It is a basic fundamental that should be taught in Little League and reinforced at every level, yet it isn't.

Too many players these days are interested in getting the big hit or driving in the big runs. Ignoring bunting and playing small ball is a practice that is filtering down to the lowest of levels, including youth baseball. But bunting can put runners in scoring position and afford teammates the opportunity to drive them in.

A player cannot bunt, though, if she doesn't know how to hold the bat. It's a simple concept that can be easily taught. While we usually advocate watching the professionals do it, so many players today simply struggle with bunting.

The Grip

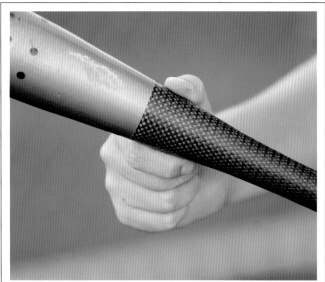

- The position of the thumb on the top hand is very important.

- The batter should make a loose fist with her thumb sticking straight into the air. The thumb will provide a place against which the bat can rest and it will keep the bat from flying out of the hitter's hand.

- As the batter moves into position to bunt, she will slide her top hand up the bat and form a cradle.

The Cradle

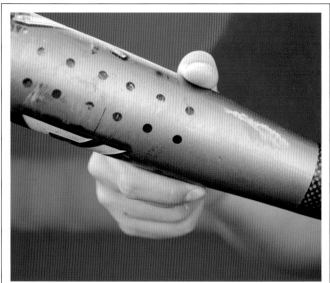

- Have the batter form a cradle with her thumb, forefinger, and the rest of her hand on which the bat will rest.

- The batter should apply some force with the thumb to hold the bat in place but not too much. She shouldn't be pushing with her top hand until she makes contact with the ball.

- The cradle should be slightly spongy. The batter shouldn't be forcing the ball back from where it came, and if she has some flexibility in her grip, she won't.

So it is up to you to teach them the fundamentals and drive them home, beginning with the grip. A proper bunting grip is easy to achieve, but so is an improper one. While a proper grip can bring about great success, an improper one can cause serious injury. If a player is not holding the bat properly during a bunt, she can easily get one of her fingers smashed by a pitch. Broken fingers are a common result of inadequate bunting skills. So make sure your players are warned repeatedly about how to hold the bat and how to make contact without risking injury.

Bunting is fluid and effective when done properly and can often yield tremendous results. When a batter cannot hold the bat properly during an attempted bunt, it is awkward and messy. Don't let your players be messy. Teach them how to hold the bat and bunt properly.

Be Careful

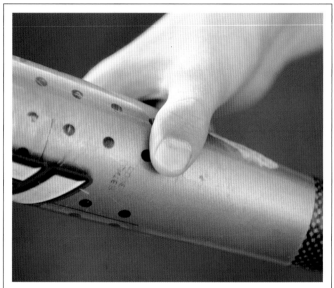

- A common mistake among youngsters is wrapping the thumb over the top of the bat when gripping it to bunt.

- This is a dangerous habit. Fingers can get broken or severely bruised if hit by a pitch. Instruct the batter to keep the cradle firm without dropping her thumb over the top of the bat.

- The batter should also use the bat to shield the lower part of her hand as much as possible.

The Bottom Hand

- The bottom hand is often the forgotten hand when it comes to bunting.

- Placement of the bottom hand varies from player to player. Some like to keep it at the knob, which will be beneficial when extended to bunt an outside pitch.

- Sliding the hand a few inches up from the knob, however, will allow the bunter more bat control. Either way, this grip will be more firm than that of the top hand.

73

POSITIONING

There are two easy-to-use methods of bunting that youngsters can learn quickly

Okay, so you have decided to start teaching the art of bunting and have already covered how to hold the bat. But how about standing in the batter's box? That is another matter entirely. As was the case when teaching hitting, individual variation is not something that should be encouraged at a young age.

Teaching a young player how to bunt is difficult enough without having to worry about some of your players trying different techniques and methods without any structure. Stick with the basics and drill them until the players can perform them in their sleep. It will only serve them well as they get older and begin to play in more advanced leagues.

Squaring Around Method

- This is the more traditional method of bunting and gives a clear signal to the fielders that the batter intends to bunt.

- The batter brings his front foot back and has both feet open and parallel to the pitcher.

- The body is facing the pitcher and both feet are aligned in the batter's box about at the midway point of home plate.

- The feet should be shoulder width apart.

Have Balance

- The batter's weight should be forward, on the balls of the feet with the knees slightly bent.

- The bat should be positioned out in front of the batter with the bat almost at a 45-degree angle.

- The top of the bat should be above the bottom half of the bat.

- This position limits the choices a batter has. If he does not wish to offer at the pitch, the bat should be pulled back to the body.

Much like how we approached teaching hitting, you must explain to the players that as they get older, more experienced, and become better ballplayers, they will be able to experiment a little with their stance while trying to find one that is comfortable for them. Initially, though, the positioning when teaching bunting should be limited to the basics—your basics.

Let them know right away that their choices are limited but that they do have choices. If you favor one method over another, then by all means, stress teaching that method. But what works for one player might not work for another, so be prepared to understand both the pivoting and the squaring around method, working with each individual to learn what works best for that person.

Whichever method you employ, teaching it takes time. Younger players do not always have the type of coordination needed to perform the footwork in the batter's box required during the attempted bunt. Be patient with them and go over each step carefully and frequently, making sure they have a firm grasp on the material before moving on.

The Pivoting Method

- This method adds some deception to the attempted bunt because it does not telegraph the hitter's intentions the way squaring around does.

- The batter takes his position in the box normally, but as the pitcher goes into the windup the batter pivots on the balls of the feet, bringing the bat out in front of the body.

- Much of the hitter's weight and balance will shift to the front foot. The batter will appear to be leaning into the pitch.

Final Thoughts

- As with squaring around, the knees should be slightly bent.

- This method allows for the batter to pull the bat back and take an actual swing at the ball. This can often be effective because the infielders are now charging expecting a bunt and it is easier to drive the ball past them.

- The batter can easily pull the bat back and swing because the feet have not moved far from the original stance.

MAKING CONTACT
Learning how to make contact consistently can take some time

It is essential for the batter to make contact without taking unnecessary chances during a bunt attempt. There are just some pitches that cannot be bunted, but when the pitch is in the zone, the hitter should not waste the opportunity. That's why practicing the bunt is important.

Never assume that you have done enough work with your players. Like batting practice, bunting when the coach is throwing is much different from game situations when something is actually at stake. Younger players tend to forget what they have been taught or get nervous and are unable to implement what the coach has shown them, so the best way to prevent this from happening is repetition.

Have the players bunt over and over again. Take as much time as you need with this drill because you want it to become second nature in game situations. You don't want your players at the plate flailing away at a pitch when attempting to

Don't Squeeze

- When looking to make contact, bunters need to treat the bat like gold, not a lemon. They should not squeeze it with the top hand.

- Instruct bunters to simply let the bat rest in the cradle and look to make contact, guiding the bat where they want it to go.

- The bottom hand acts as the rudder, holding the bat steady as the top hand guides it into position to receive the ball.

Point to the Sky

- The bat is kept tilted upward as it is moved forward to make contact with the ball.

- The top hand should always remain above the bottom hand when bunting.

- If the bat is kept parallel to the ground, the bunt will usually result in a popup.

- The bat should be in front of the hitter and over the plate in order to make contact with the pitch.

move a runner over. It is important to make contact regardless of whether the hitter has telegraphed his intentions or not.

If the runner takes off on the pitch expecting the ball to be bunted and the hitter has simply watched the pitch or not made contact, then the runner will likely get thrown out.

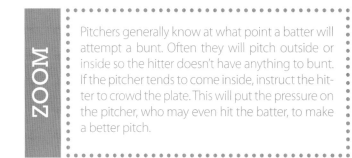
BUNTING

Patience

- The batter must be patient and wait for the pitch to arrive. Instruct players to avoid thrusting the bat at the ball.

- Think of the bat as being rubbery. The ball will use the momentum of hitting the wood (or aluminum) and propel itself back out onto the field. It doesn't need help when attempting to sacrifice. The batter should simply use the bat as a directional signal for which way he intends the ball to go.

No Lunging

- If the batter has been instructed to only swing at strikes, then why would bunting be any different?

- Batters should not lunge at outside pitches or reach for pitches above the head or out of the strike zone.

- Bad pitches are difficult to bunt, and the batter is more likely not to move the runner over if he lunges at a pitch out of the strike zone.

BUNTING FOR BASE HITS
Who says that all base hits have to be line drives?

The saying "They are all line drives in the box score" never had more meaning than when applying it to bunting for a base hit. This aspect of the game requires a great deal of practice, skill, knowledge and understanding of the game, determination, and most of all speed.

Coaches need to recognize early who their fastest runners are and have them work on their bunting skills. For a speedy player, the bunt base hit is an excellent way to get on base,

particularly if the hitter is capable of placing the ball wherever he wants with the bat. If a player with speed can drop a bunt in the no-man's land close to the baselines when the infield is back, more often than not it will result in a hit.

Talk to your players, though, because they don't have to be speed demons to be sneaky. Generally, you won't be asking your cleanup hitter to drop down a bunt. But when any of your hitters step into the batter's box, have them take note of

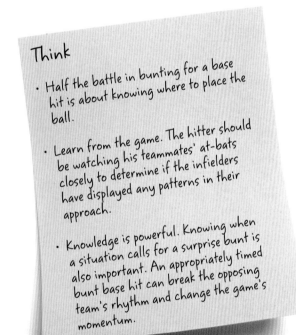

Think

• Half the battle in bunting for a base hit is about knowing where to place the ball.

• Learn from the game. The hitter should be watching his teammates' at-bats closely to determine if the infielders have displayed any patterns in their approach.

• Knowledge is powerful. Knowing when a situation calls for a surprise bunt is also important. An appropriately timed bunt base hit can break the opposing team's rhythm and change the game's momentum.

Stay Back

• Staying in the regular batting stance as long as possible is key to the element of surprise. This is where knowing the game and knowing the right time to bunt comes into play.

• Right-handed batters should take a short step toward first base as they begin the process of bunting but make sure they remain in the batter's box; otherwise they could be called out if they make contact.

where the fielders are positioned. If the first and third baseman are playing even with or behind the base, then it will take them a second or two longer to get to the ball if the batter surprises them and drops down a bunt. That extra second or two is all that many hitters will need to get down the baseline and beat out a base hit.

This is something that takes work, though, and lots of it. Learning where and how to drop a bunt is not something that a player can master on a few pitches in batting practice. It takes hours of repetition to learn how to control the bat

and move out of the regular batting stance at the last possible second to ensure surprise.

Placement

- Ideally, the right-handed hitter will almost turn his bat inward toward the third baseman in an effort to get the ball down the third base line.

- The right-handed hitter can also use the gap between the pitcher and the first baseman to push a bunt toward the second baseman if he is playing back far enough.

- The hitter should make sure the bunt travels far enough away from the catcher to be effective.

Avoid the Pitcher

- The hitter should not push the ball back to the mound. He is wasting the at-bat if the ball cannot be bunted up either line for a base hit.

- The pitcher should be the only fielder with a chance to get to the ball if it is bunted for a base hit properly. The hitter should make him work to get it.

- The batter should see which way the pitcher falls off the mound and attempt to put the ball in the no-man's land opposite of that.

79

BUNTING FOR LEFTIES
Left-handed batters are in a better position to bunt for a base hit

If you coach older players and you have some on your team that hit left-handed, know how to handle a bat, and are fast, treat them well. These players will be of great benefit to you as a coach and of great benefit to the team.

But before you hand these players a bat, turn them loose, and say "Go start bunting for base hits," you have to work with them. While this applies to right-handed hitters as well, lefties, particularly those that will be hitting at the top of the batting order, need to have a better understanding of what is going on, not only within the context of a particular game but conceptually as well.

There's nothing quite like having a left-handed speedster at the top of the lineup beat out a bunt. It can do several things, including forcing the defense to rush and make a bad throw. This could lead to an error, and instead of having a man on first you have one on second or third.

Pushing

- Bunting the ball down the third base line allows the left-handed batter a bit more time because the third baseman has a longer throw than if the ball were hit on the first base side.

- The left-handed hitter almost appears to be throwing his bat at the ball when sending it down to third base. This actually requires a great deal of bat control and touch so as not to bunt it too hard or into foul territory.

Pulling

- When a left-handed hitter pulls a bunt down the first base line, it is often called a drag bunt.

- The batter almost turns his body and begins to move before the ball is hit, but times it perfectly to begin moving as the ball makes contact with the bat, giving the appearance that he is running beforehand.

- This is an effective way to pick up a base hit against a right-handed pitcher.

Too many coaches today don't employ this philosophy, though, because they do not believe their players are capable or old enough to grasp the significance of a well-placed bunt. That's where you, as a coach, must drill your players, at least at every practice and perhaps even every day.

Take those lefties aside every day for ten or fifteen minutes before practice and work on their footwork in the batter's box. Drill them on the art of surprise and situational hitting where bunting for a base hit is appropriate. Good left-handed bunters are special commodities. Those players, however, aren't solely responsible for managing their own talent. It's up to the coach to nurture them and bring it out.

Stay Planted

- Though there is a great deal of motion when bunting left-handed, it is important to remind your players to keep their feet planted in the batter's box as long as possible.

- If the left-handed batter begins running before the ball is bunted, one of two things could happen. He could be called out for hitting the ball outside of the batter's box. He could also lose control of the bat because he is so worried about running.

A Weapon

- A good left-handed bunter is a weapon that should not be ignored or misused.

- While bunting is not easy, making contact on a bunt is easier than when swinging for a hit. Working on bunting for base hits with a left-hander who is a weak hitter can build confidence.

- A good bunter can be a huge disruption to the defense.

THE SQUEEZE

The squeeze play is risky but well worth the gamble if executed properly

If you are going to coach young players about the game, then be prepared to coach them about all aspects of it. This includes the sacrifice and suicide squeeze. The sacrifice squeeze (or "safety squeeze") works as any other sacrifice bunt would, but the suicide squeeze means that the runner is heading home regardless of what happens at the plate.

Far too often coaches on every level eschew the sacrifice or the squeeze in favor of looking for a base hit. While this happens often in the Major Leagues (particularly the American League), it is happening with increasing frequency in youth baseball simply because coaches do not bother to teach their players what to do in such situations.

Communication

- The batter, the runner, and the third base coach must all be on the same page and aware that the squeeze is coming.

- If the batter misses the sign and swings away, then the results could be disastrous. The runner could sustain serious injuries when barreling down the line thinking a squeeze play is on if the batter swings normally. The possibility of the runner getting hit with the bat or ball makes communication and understanding the signs essential.

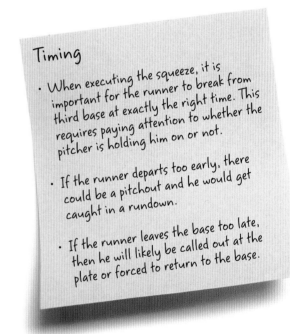

Timing

- When executing the squeeze, it is important for the runner to break from third base at exactly the right time. This requires paying attention to whether the pitcher is holding him on or not.

- If the runner departs too early, there could be a pitchout and he would get caught in a rundown.

- If the runner leaves the base too late, then he will likely be called out at the plate or forced to return to the base.

Youngsters aren't taught and drilled enough on bunting in general, but when it comes to the squeeze play there is practically no instruction. While some would say bunting is not allowed in some leagues, that is a shallow answer. Teach the game completely, all of it. Would you accept an English teacher ignoring spelling because children can now use computers that have spell-check? Not likely, so don't ignore part of the game simply because some of your younger players won't be put in a position to use what you have taught them. It will serve them at some point during their years of playing the game.

The most important aspect of the squeeze is that your players understand that contact must be made when the suicide squeeze is on. Bunt the ball, anywhere. If it goes foul then there's no harm. If it's bunted to an infielder, at least there will be a play at the plate. But if no contact is made the runner is on his own. So stress contact when teaching the suicide squeeze and emphasize your preference for contacting when discussing the sacrifice squeeze. Either way, teach the squeeze.

Tips

- It is easier for the runner if the batter is right-handed because he will block the catcher's view for a split second, allowing the runner to get down the line a bit easier.

- Instruct your runner to move on third base and be as disruptive as possible. Because the squeeze is used so infrequently, the pitcher could get rattled and throw a wild pitch that would allow the runner to score.

Nerves

- The squeeze can be a tension-filled experience for some youngsters. Don't let it be.

- Encourage them and make them feel confident in their abilities. Treat it as you would a normal bunt. The results of a squeeze play

may provide a bit of a different result but the concept is the same.

- Block out the runner, catcher, umpire, and everyone else on the field once it has been determined the squeeze play is on.

TAKING THE FIELD
Catching is a difficult but rewarding position to master

When organizing a youth baseball team, finding someone to be the catcher is usually the toughest part. Traditionally coaches have put the biggest kid or the slowest kid back behind the plate. but the truth of the matter is that few kids actually want to catch. There's too much anonymity in catching, too much can go wrong, and it is too easy to sustain an injury, either from a bat, a batted ball, or a collision.

It is also hot and difficult to see out of the mask. Very often each team has only one mask and they aren't one size fits all, so it's easy to understand that from a child's point of view, catching is a necessary evil.

But as the coach, it is your responsibility to stamp out all these myths about catching. The person behind the plate is one of the most important if not the most important player on the field. He's involved in every single pitch of every single game. He calls the game when older kids are playing, he

Getting in Position

- The catcher takes up position in the chalked-out box behind the plate, far enough away from the hitter so that he will not get hit with a bat but not so far that he is out of the box.

- The catcher should stand with the feet just inside shoulder width apart, checking and adjusting the equipment if needed before crouching down into a squat. The right foot should be back slightly.

Weight Distribution

- More than half of the catcher's body weight should be on the front part or the balls of the feet.

- Having the majority of the weight on the front part of the feet will help balance and allow the catcher to spring up and out to make a play or a throw much easier than if he were flat-footed or had more weight resting on the heels.

keeps the pitcher calm, and most importantly, if he weren't there, the ball would just roll right to the backstop.

A little humor and a big dose of information about how important the position is certainly don't hurt when recruiting a backstop.

Glove Positioning

- When the catcher is giving signals prior to a pitch, the glove hand and arm usually rest on the left thigh, helping prevent the batter or opposing third base coach from getting a clear view of the signals.

- When the catcher is preparing to receive a pitch, the glove hand should be up and away from the body, though the elbow should be bent slightly so there is some give to the glove and hand when receiving the pitch.

The Throwing Hand

- The throwing hand must be protected from foul tips, which can split fingers or break bones.

- If the bases are empty, the catcher should keep the throwing hand behind the back, open but relaxed.

- Another common practice is to have the throwing hand clenched in a fist, placing it behind the glove so that the catcher has two hands available should a pitch go awry.

RECEIVING THE BALL
Setting a proper target and receiving the ball well are basic skills every catcher needs

Sometimes receiving the ball is not always that easy for a young catcher. Young pitchers are often wild and have little control over where their pitches will end up, making a game or practice very trying for the catcher.

The catcher, however, can make things easier on the pitcher by simply setting a proper, steady target. Stress to your catcher the importance of keeping the glove in place and the target true. If the pitcher sees the glove moving left or right, up or down, then chances are her pitch will miss the target. A strong catcher who sets up well and presents a solid target can be of great benefit to the pitcher. This kind of catcher can settle a pitcher down and help her throw strikes.

Setting a Target

- Setting a target is very often called framing a pitch. That means the catcher is setting up a square in which he wants the pitch to end up after it is thrown.

- The catcher should present a firm and consistent target. That means keeping the glove hand steady. He should not wave or waggle the glove because it will have an impact on where and how the pitcher delivers the ball.

Glove Direction

- It is important for the catcher to use his glove as any other player on the field would despite the differences between it and, say, an infielder's glove.

- Proper glove direction and receiving starts with proper body positioning. If the catcher is off balance or teetering in any way, the positioning of the glove will change and this could lead to dropped pitches or passed balls.

Setting a proper target and actually catching the ball are two different things. You need to make sure that you have a catcher who isn't afraid behind the plate. If the catcher is fearful of getting hit with the bat or frightened that he might miss the pitch, then that person is not the one you want catching.

This is a position of confidence and leadership. That begins with confidence in one's own ability. The catcher needs to be surehanded and believe that he will catch every pitch. This is particularly important when molding young catchers. Far too often, you see catchers in games involving younger children continuously running to the backstop after missing a pitch. While some of that has to do with the pitcher, most of the time the catcher has not done the job properly.

Look for a catcher who not only wants to be behind the plate, but also has the ability to be back there. The primary responsibility of the catcher is to receive or catch the ball. If that skill is lacking, you need another catcher.

Glove Direction II

- When receiving a high pitch, the fingers should be pointed upward with the palm facing out toward the pitcher.

- When receiving a low pitch, the fingers should be pointing downward with the palm up as if to scoop up a handful of dirt.

- Outside pitches could be received in the same fashion an infielder makes plays, either going to the backhand or extending the arm to catch it normally.

The Outside Pitch

- If a pitch is so far outside that a backhand snag isn't possible, then the catcher must step out to receive it or slide over on the balls of the feet.

- The catcher should never lunge for the ball. He should move with the pitch rather than diving at it.

- If the pitch is too far outside or inside and there is no chance of catching it, the catcher should turn and prepare to catch it off the backstop.

BLOCKING LOW PITCHES
Blocking pitches in the dirt in front of the plate can save a pitcher

Trying to catch or block a low pitch is probably the greatest challenge that a catcher faces. When a ball hits the ground it becomes unpredictable, squirting in every direction but the one the catcher expects. Add in the fact that most young pitchers are wild to begin with and the task of trying to harness that wildness only becomes that much more difficult.

Unlike reflexes or arm strength or speed, learning how to block a low pitch is something that can be taught. Work with

your young catchers, showing them how to flop inverted V style when the pitch is in front of them. Show them how to move laterally to block a low pitch and work with them to improve their technique.

This is an aspect of the catcher's game that can improve greatly with practice and effort. It will take work on your end too. The catcher will need a competent partner to work with, and that's where the coach comes in. While you and the

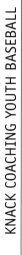

Knees Please

- It is imperative that low pitches do not get by the catcher, particularly when there are runners on base.

- The catcher should drop to his knees and attempt to block the ball. Catching the ball isn't as much of an issue as blocking it is.

- If a catcher doesn't catch the ball, a runner could advance. If the ball is blocked, however, the runner will likely not attempt to take another base.

The Glove

- Catchers should use the glove as a tool, catching the ball if they can, but using the glove as another implement to block an errant pitch.

- The glove should be slammed down on the ground quickly between

the catcher's legs lest a low pitch bounce between the legs before the body collapses.

- Advise catchers not to try to scoop the ball out of the dirt. The pitches are usually too unpredictable.

catcher are working on making these improvements in her game, remind her of just how important an aspect of catching blocking a pitch is. It can save runs and help preserve a pitcher's confidence.

Outside/Inside Pitches

- Depending on how far outside the pitch is, the catcher has two options: Slide and drop to the knees in an attempt to block it, or if the pitch is far enough outside, take an actual step up and out to catch it.

- Inside pitches generally can be a bit more complicated because the batter can get in the way. Usually a slide to the inside will be enough to stop an inside pitch. If it goes too far inside, it might hit the batter or simply skip on back to the wall.

Blocking Drills

- The catcher kneels behind home plate, in full equipment, while a coach heads to a spot halfway to the mound with a bucket of balls.

- The coach proceeds to throw the balls at varying speeds so that they bounce in front of the catcher and he is forced to use the body to block the pitch. This drill is carried out in a rapid-fire manner and will help improve the catcher's reflexes and mobility.

THROWING OUT BASERUNNERS

Catchers shouldn't be discouraged if they struggle to throw out baserunners

Most catchers are not going to throw out a large percentage of runners attempting to steal. It's a fact and there is no shame in that. The pitch has to be perfect, the throw has to be perfect, and the shortstop or second baseman has to be ready to catch the ball and apply the tag at precisely the right time for the runner to be called out.

This perfect storm of events does not happen very often, and because of that the catcher usually bears the brunt of the blame. Your job as coach is to get that notion right out of your catcher's head. There is no blame. Explain how difficult throwing out a runner is. Consider that in 2008 Jose Molina threw out thirty-three of the seventy-five runners

The Throwing Hand

- There are two schools of thought regarding the bare hand. The first involves keeping the throwing hand behind the back and whipping it out and around prior to making the throw.

- The second involves keeping the bare hand balled into a fist behind the glove,

which cuts out precious seconds when making the transfer for the throw.

- Either method is acceptable, but comfort level and personal preference are important factors.

The Squat

- Being able to catch and throw the ball out of the squat takes a very strong, accurate arm.

- Often, catchers who are capable of making such a throw do so while falling to their knees.

- Having a quick release and throwing from a squat is also beneficial for throwing behind a runner at first in an attempted pickoff.

- While this method can be effective and surprising, it is not recommended.

who attempted to steal to lead the Major Leagues. That's a 44 percent success rate for the catcher.

It's easy to see why a catcher would get discouraged when seeing those kinds of results. Explain to your catcher that success is often measured in more than statistics. Sometimes the runner is just too fast to catch. Sometimes the infielder won't catch the ball or apply the tag properly. Remind him that if they keep doing the job properly, using the correct form and technique, then there is nothing more they can do.

Hall of Famer Johnny Bench was one of the most influential catchers in the history of the game. He popularized the one-handed style of catching in the late 60s and early 70s, keeping his throwing hand behind his back, safe from foul tips. He had a cannon for an arm and bragged of how he could throw accurately to twice the distance between home and second base.

Jump and Throw

- This is the most popular method and the easiest for a young catcher to master.

- As the catcher receives the ball, he moves quickly, springing up and planting the right foot.

- Most of the body should be perpendicular to second base. The arms should be brought up into a throwing motion as the catcher jumps up.

- The catcher then strides and throws. This method allows for using the momentum of the jump when throwing to second base.

The Pitchout

- Make sure the pitcher and the catcher have communicated that there will be a pitchout during the at-bat. The last thing a coach wants is for a pitcher to throw a ball outside and not have the catcher there to catch it.

- As the pitcher goes into the windup, the catcher steps out to receive the throw.

CATCHING POPUPS
Catching a popup can be confusing and difficult for catchers

The catcher has a distinct disadvantage over the rest of his teammates when attempting to catch a pop fly. Not only does the catcher wear a mask and or a helmet, he has several pounds of equipment with which to deal, making mobility an issue.

Therefore, the catcher needs to be coordinated in terms of discarding the mask, locating the ball, and lumbering around with shinguards and a chest protector. It isn't easy but with

practice a catcher can become quite accomplished.

This is where you come in. Find your fungo bat and get to work. Hit popup after popup to your catcher. Run the drill over and over again. When you think you have done it enough times, hit a few more popups to be sure. The last thing you want during a game is to have your catcher drop a popup and have the batter get new life because of the error.

This can be a fun drill for both you and your catcher. Hit the

The Mask

- Taking off the mask is an essential part of catching a popup. It is much easier to see the ball and follow its flight with the mask off.

- The catcher should grab the mask from the bottom and pull it up and off his head. It may be more difficult with

the hockey-style helmet so he should practice removing the mask for several minutes a day.

- The catcher should throw the mask in the direction opposite the ball so it cannot be tripped over.

Positioning

- The corner infielders and the pitcher will have priority over the catcher when calling for a popup in the infield around home plate. They are coming into the ball and have a better angle.

- The catcher should position himself under the ball with his back to the infield. This way as the ball drifts toward the infield, he is backing up with it and not chasing it.

popups near the plate, near the dugout, near the wall, and by the mound. Have the player move around. Challenge him to catch the ball and get better each time. If your catcher is competitive enough, he'll respond to the challenge.

Catching the Ball

- Once the catcher has picked up the flight of the ball, the player should hold his glove just below eye level and watch its path above the top of the glove.

- The catcher should settle under the ball with the glove extended slightly at a height where the player can still track the ball's path.

- The catcher should use two hands and be prepared to pull the ball out of the glove and be ready to throw if there is a runner on base.

The Wall

- Often popups behind the plate will drift into the wall or the screen. The catcher should be aware of where the screen/wall is and avoid running into it.

- The catcher should approach the wall much like an outfielder would, arm outstretched.

- Another safe and effective method on shorter popups at the screen involves sliding feet first into the wall while watching the ball's flight. The equipment will protect the catcher from injury.

FIELDING BUNTS
Good reflexes are essential in order to field a bunt properly

As this chapter has progressed, we've been talking about building the perfect catcher. The player needs to be able to catch, have a strong arm, and be confident behind the plate. As is the case when dealing with runners attempting to steal, fielding a bunt also involves anticipation.

The perfect catcher also needs good reflexes. The catcher needs to be able to spring out from behind the plate quickly, efficiently, and effortlessly in order to field the bunt. Now, size

shouldn't matter when it comes to reflexes. Big catchers have been known to move quickly.

What matters is a player's ability to pounce on the bunt and come up throwing accurately. Not every catcher is capable of performing this task. Some catchers are simply too slow or do not have the footwork. When searching for a catcher, finding one with strong reflexes will only enhance the package.

The techniques involved with fielding a bunt can be taught

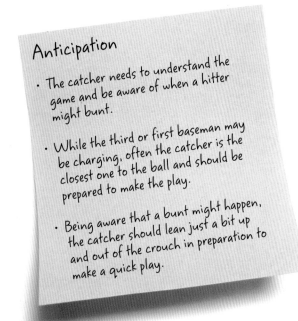

Anticipation

- The catcher needs to understand the game and be aware of when a hitter might bunt.

- While the third or first baseman may be charging, often the catcher is the closest one to the ball and should be prepared to make the play.

- Being aware that a bunt might happen, the catcher should lean just a bit up and out of the crouch in preparation to make a quick play.

The Route

- Ideally the catcher should be quick enough to remove the mask while springing out from behind the plate.

- The catcher should take a bit of a circular route to the ball if it's bunted to third. This will allow him to be in a better position to throw to first or second base after making the play.

- A direct line to the ball is also acceptable, but it involves having to spin to make the throw to first or second base.

to anyone. Quickness can be improved, though, through practice. If you have a slower catcher who tends to lumber rather than pounce, put in the time after practice. Roll dribbler after dribbler in front of the plate and drill him on the proper routes to the ball, the correct principles regarding fielding it, and coming up throwing and trusting their teammates.

Fielding a bunt is not difficult but it is involved. While quick reflexes and great anticipatory skills would certainly be of tremendous benefit to every catcher when attempting to field a bunt, these skills can be brought up to acceptable levels with extra work and attention from the coach.

Catchers are unique individuals. They aren't born to be catchers; they are molded into them. The ones that have good reflexes are simply easier to mold.

Watching the Ball

- The catcher's primary concern when fielding a bunt is the ball, not the runner.

- The catcher should not take his eyes off the ball to check the runner. Bunts are unpredictable, and during the split second it takes to check the runner, the catcher could lose sight of the ball.

- Watching the ball until it is in the glove is important. Once the catcher has fielded the ball, he can worry about the runner and making the throw.

Listen

- Since the catcher is watching the ball, someone needs to be watching the runner.

- Usually the pitcher or one of the corner infielders will follow the runner and let the catcher know where the play is to be made.

- The catcher needs to *listen* to his teammates, who will shout to which base the catcher needs to be throwing. It is important the pitcher and infielders understand they must communicate with the catcher.

CALLING A GAME
The catcher is the guide who leads the pitcher through a game

A coach has a wonderful opportunity to be a teacher when working with a young catcher, especially one that shows promise. Explaining how to "call a game"—which essentially means the catcher is directing the pitcher in a two-man play—and watching his charge pick up on the nuances of working her way through a batting order is one of the more rewarding aspects of coaching.

It is important for you as a coach, when dealing with older players, to discuss the game with your pitchers and catchers. They are a separate breed and should have a different understanding of how the game progresses. The other position players will have a certain feel for the game, but the pitcher and the catcher operate largely in a vacuum during the game, working hand in hand with much of the responsibility falling on the catcher.

A common practice is to have the coach call the pitches

The Signs

- The catcher and the pitcher must go over the signals so that when the catcher flashes a sign, the pitcher will know what pitch to throw.

- The catcher puts fingers down to indicate what

pitch he thinks should be thrown—one finger for fastball, two fingers for a curveball, three for a slider, etc. There are no steadfast rules for signals. It should be whatever works best for the pitcher and the catcher.

Learn the Hitters

- Older players who face an opponent more than once should begin studying the hitters they face.

- Catchers, like pitchers, need to learn a hitter's tendencies and remember which pitches worked the last time the two teams faced. It's a good idea to write these facts down and keep a book that can be referred to prior to each meeting with a specific team.

- Catchers should share the information with the pitcher.

from the bench. Try not to do that, especially if you have a catcher who is intelligent enough to guide a pitching staff. At this age, there won't be many of them, but there are some special players out there who study the game and have a good sense of working the hitter and how to guide a pitcher through any rough patches that might arise.

A good catcher will know when to be emphatic in calling a pitch and when to back off and let the pitcher decide what to throw. Often pitchers are stubborn and rely on ego rather than common sense during the pitch selection process.

Catchers don't have that problem. They are simply working their way through an opposing lineup and don't care much about showing off a fastball.

So work with your catcher and let her grow in the position. Explain the ins and outs of calling a game and let the catcher take that knowledge and expand on it.

Taking Charge

- A catcher should be able to work with a pitcher. It's a special relationship, particularly when it's obvious the pitcher and the catcher are in sync.

- Though the catcher works with the pitcher, he needs to be the one taking charge on the field, especially if he is working with a younger or more inexperienced pitcher.

- Catchers should be aggressive in calling the game and use the knowledge gained by studying hitters to guide the pitcher through the outing.

Changing Speeds

- Part of calling a game is knowing when to throw certain pitches at certain times.

- A good catcher will have his pitcher change speeds and set hitters up.

- Catchers should not give the batter a steady diet of fastballs. They should work some off-speed pitches into the mix to keep the batter guessing.

- Catchers need to set up both inside and outside and avoid always staying behind the center of the plate so pitch location becomes predictable.

FRAMING THE ZONE
An older catcher needs to be skilled at presenting a proper target

While we went over this subject briefly in the previous chapter, it is worth a more in-depth look when discussing older players and how they evolve as catchers. As a young catcher, it is important to simply present a steady and stable target. But that's about all a young catcher really needs to be concerned with, because most of the time the pitchers in the earlier age groups are so wild, the nuance of framing a pitch does not really apply.

Presenting a steady, stable target is also a prerequisite to catching when your players get older. But once they learn how to call a game and become involved in the intricacies of setting up hitters, working both sides of the plate and varying the speed of the pitches, it becomes imperative that they learn about how that is all impacted by the target they present and how it is presented.

A good catcher can influence the umpire with the way he

Set the Target

- The older catcher and pitcher can work more of a finesse game with the catcher setting up a target on the black (the edge of the plate).

- Working the corners is risky, but the battery can determine early in a game what the umpire's tendencies are

and adjust their game plan accordingly.

- Catchers should not give up working the corners if they don't get a few early calls. He should keep picking away at the black and testing the umpire.

The Drag

- This is probably the most difficult aspect of framing a target and getting the umpire to actually call a ball a strike.

- After catching a ball off the plate, in as subtle a manner as possible the catcher should drag his glove back

over the plate and hold it there for a split second.

- Very often the umpire will make a call based not on where the pitch crosses the plate, but where the catcher's glove is after the pitch is thrown.

98

sets up his target. He can help create the illusion that a pitch is a strike despite the fact that the pitch may be off the outside or the inside corner of the plate.

Of course there will be times when the umpire will not take the bait and bite when the catcher drags the ball back over the plate after it has been caught. But once a catcher has established a reputation for being good defensively, that reputation will carry a great deal of weight with the umpires. It works the same way with hitters who have reputations for being patient at the plate. If *they* are taking a pitch, it must be a ball. If the catcher has framed the pitch as a strike, it *must* be a strike.

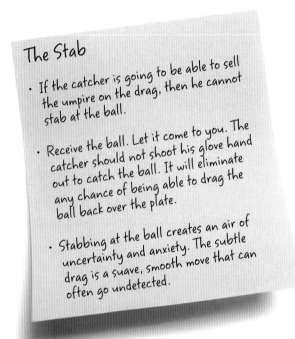

The Stab

- If the catcher is going to be able to sell the umpire on the drag, then he cannot stab at the ball.

- Receive the ball. Let it come to you. The catcher should not shoot his glove hand out to catch the ball. It will eliminate any chance of being able to drag the ball back over the plate.

- Stabbing at the ball creates an air of uncertainty and anxiety. The subtle drag is a suave, smooth move that can often go undetected.

Balance

- Having good form and proper balance is also a big part of framing and implementing the drag.

- Staying too low or too high in the crouch will lead to wobbling or lunging when receiving the ball.

- If the catcher is not steady when receiving a pitch, then it likely will not matter where it has been framed because it won't be called a strike.

PITCHOUTS
Knowing when to call a pitchout can be an effective tool in a catcher's arsenal

Having spent so much time discussing learning about the game, studying it and understanding the little things that go into having a high baseball IQ, it only seems logical that we add the pitchout to that list.

The physical part of conducting a pitchout is simple enough—stand, step, and throw. But the good catchers are the ones who have studied the opposition and understand their pitchers. The good catchers are the ones who recognize how a game has taken shape; they understand momentum and realize that a stolen base by the opposition could be devastating. It is at that point when a good catcher will decide to call for a pitchout.

Anticipation

- Knowing when to call a pitchout is important.

- Anticipating what the runner is thinking and knowing when she may run are paramount for a catcher.

- Make sure the catcher and the pitcher are on the same page when calling for a pitchout.

- Work with your pitcher to make sure he understands how to mask a pitchout and prevent a runner from picking it up.

The Runner

- The catcher should always keep an eye on the runner. He should glance over at him before each pitch and after every pitch to make sure he is staying put.

- The catcher shouldn't be afraid to throw down to first behind the runner as a prelude to a pitchout.

- If the catcher has committed to the pitchout, he should take one final look at the runner before the pitcher goes into the windup.

Pitchouts are not like throws over to first to keep the runner close. They are counted as balls, so calling for two or three of them against one batter is not advisable. So use discretion when calling for a pitchout. Generally, the pitchout is effective to help prevent the opposition's speedier players from getting an edge on the bases. If a catcher senses that the runner will be taking off with the pitch, then a pitchout is in order.

Some players are simply too fast and will steal a base regardless of whether a pitchout has been called. Tip your hat to them and move on. For the most part, though, players have a difficult time stealing on a pitchout.

One thing to remember as well: Once a pitchout has been called, odds are the catcher will not call for another on the next pitch. That is when the runner will usually take off. Surprise the runner every once in a while. Have your catcher call for back-to-back pitchouts just in case. It will make the game more interesting and let the runner know that your catcher means business.

The Step

- The catcher has to sell the pitchout by staying in a crouch as long as possible before receiving the ball.

- He stands up and steps out toward first base with the right foot if the batter is right-handed.

- If the batter is left-handed, he steps out with the left foot and pivots while doing so into the throwing position. The body should be positioned perpendicular to second base.

The Throw

- The catcher has the element of surprise because he knows the pitchout is coming. He should use that advantage and take his time with the throw.

- Work on the pitchout for several minutes after every practice session. It will get catchers in the habit of making the throw from the standing position, which is slightly different than the throw coming out of a crouch on a stolen base.

TEAM LEADER
The catcher is often regarded as the grit and guts of the team

Every team needs a leader. It needs someone to take charge on and off the field, someone who is vocal, charismatic, and can pull the group together when needed. The catcher is often that player and with good reason.

The catcher is involved in every pitch, every play in one way or another regardless of whether she ever touches the ball. The catcher is the only one who can see each and every play unfold in front of her, thus having a better sense of what's going on in the game than any other player on the field. While it may seem like a bit much to put this kind of pressure on a younger player, it really isn't.

If a younger player has shown a predisposition to catching, then she has already demonstrated that she can handle more than the other players can. Catching is a huge responsibility, and if a player is willing to take on that responsibility then it says a great deal about what you can expect of them.

Take Charge

- The catcher is the field general, taking charge of the game from behind the plate.

- The catcher not only calls a game but also aligns the defense. He will step out from behind the plate at any given point in the game and signal his teammates as to where they should be playing defensively.

- The catcher can dictate the flow of the game by how he is calling it for the pitcher and how he conducts himself behind the plate.

A Calming Voice

- The catcher is often the voice of reason for his pitcher, calming the hurler down when things are going poorly.

- A catcher must have good judgment and know when it is time to take a walk out to the mound and have a chat with her pitcher. He needs to recognize when the pitcher is losing control of himself and the game.

- The catcher should be encouraging with the pitcher, never derogatory or negative.

We are not advocating turning over the coaching reins to the catcher; that's not what this is about. But if you have a player who is eager to catch and is willing to tackle what that entails, then you as a coach need to nurture that and let that player know what comes along with being a catcher.

It takes a special player to be a leader. That player needs to be able to encourage in one breath and chastise in the next, all while not alienating his teammates. This responsibility often falls on the catcher, who has traditionally been the glue in many a clubhouse. It seems like we're making too big a deal of this, especially since we're talking about youngsters here. But leaders emerge at all levels and if one of your players has shown signs that they can lead, put them at the front of the pack and watch what happens.

Vocalize

- While it is best to keep calm when dealing with the pitcher, the catcher needs to be vocal in all other areas of the game.

- Catchers should not be afraid to bark out orders from behind the plate, shouting encouragingly to teammates when the need arises and admonishing them when necessary as well.

- The catcher should challenge teammates, and occasionally, the opposition when needed.

Vision

- You can't teach vision to a catcher. Either they have it or they don't.

- Catchers need to see the whole field, taking in every aspect of the game and analyzing it on the fly.

- They need to learn all the nuances, from positioning players, to calling a game, to understanding how to set up a batter.

- A good catcher with vision is almost like having a coach on the field.

BLOCKING THE PLATE
Using the body properly on plays at the plate is crucial

This is where a catcher's mettle is tested. It is also where you, as a coach, get to see if you made the correct decision in choosing your catcher. Blocking the plate can lead to a bone-jarring collision, which is one of the reasons why a coach will often pick the biggest kid to catch.

Size, however, will not help the catcher if he isn't smart enough to know how to use it. Blocking the plate not only takes skill, it also takes courage to step in front of a runner

knowing that you will likely get hit. Work with your catcher on certain techniques that will allow full coverage of the plate yet will hopefully prevent any serious injury.

If the catcher understands how to drop into position and does so in an aggressive manner, chances are he will come out on top of any bang-bang play at the plate. Remember that the catcher is the one wearing the equipment and is the one with all the protection.

The Left Foot

- It is important to remember that the catcher cannot block the plate if he does not have the ball.

- The catcher should be facing out into the field with the left foot on the plate.

- He should leave enough of the plate visible so the runner cannot claim it was blocked.

- Both feet should be spread apart at shoulder length in a balanced stance.

Be Square

- Depending on the accuracy of the throw, the catcher should stay planted firmly, squared up to the field where the throw and the runner will both be in sight.

- If the catcher has to move off the plate to retrieve a throw, he should move entirely off the plate if

necessary. The catcher should not stretch like a first baseman simply to get the throw.

- He must move to the ball if necessary and return to the plate as quickly as possible after catching it.

Be sure to remind your backstop to discard the mask when readying to take a throw. It will be easier to see the throw coming and prepare better for the expected impact.

Stop and Drop

- If the runner is attempting to slide and the throw has arrived at the plate first, the catcher should drop to one knee. This will present a smaller target for the runner.

- Once the catcher has the ball, blocking the plate is acceptable and encouraged—but while keeping an eye on the throw. The catcher should not be looking to drop into position to make a play while the ball is still in flight.

The Left Shin

- When down on the ground and blocking the plate, the catcher should attempt to keep the left shinguard facing out into the path of the oncoming runner.

- Remember that the catcher is the one wearing the equipment. Often a runner will not want to slide into the catcher's shinguard for fear of injuring a hand or ankle. As a result, he will attempt to go around or over the catcher. The catcher should be prepared for this possibility.

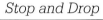
ADVANCED CATCHING

TAGGING THE RUNNER
Two hands and good positioning are required to make a proper tag

Tagging a runner at home plate can be very difficult. The runner is attempting to knock the ball out of the catcher's hands, so the catcher should be using both hands to hold the ball tightly and apply the tag. It generally makes for an awkward play on the catcher's part because flexibility is limited if the tag is made properly.

Assuming that the catcher uses both hands to apply the tag, then the catcher's reach and ability to move from the first base side of the plate into the runner is compromised. Obviously it would be easier if the catcher, after accepting a throw up the first base line, simply whirled and leaned with his glove hand into the runner.

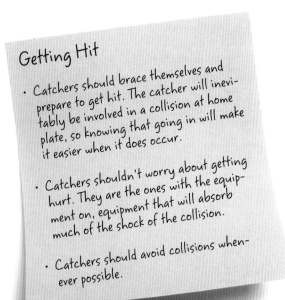

Getting Hit

- Catchers should brace themselves and prepare to get hit. The catcher will inevitably be involved in a collision at home plate, so knowing that going in will make it easier when it does occur.

- Catchers shouldn't worry about getting hurt. They are the ones with the equipment on, equipment that will absorb much of the shock of the collision.

- Catchers should avoid collisions whenever possible.

Holding the Ball

- When accepting the throw from a teammate prior to a play at the plate, the catcher should hold the ball in the glove with the throwing hand.

- This will offer maximum protection for the ball when making the tag.

- While many of the plays at the plate develop quickly, it is important for the catcher to protect the ball instinctively once it has arrived at the plate.

But that would give the runner more of an opportunity to knock the ball free. Therefore, the catcher must dive over or move his entire body to be in proper position to make the tag.

Drill your catcher on where to stand and work with the outfielders and cutoff men on making a good throw. If the cutoff man or the outfielder makes a throw up the first base line, then the catcher is left in a bad spot. Teach your players to throw to the middle of the plate or on the third base side so that the catcher will be in a better position to make a tag.

Teaching the catcher how to "fake" waiting on a throw is also beneficial. Instruct the catcher to stand stoically as if the throw isn't coming. The throw, however, will be coming and the runner will be deceived into thinking he can score easily. It's a neat little trick that isn't used often enough when applying a tag.

Tagging

- Once the ball is in the glove, the catcher should leave it there and covered with the bare hand.

- Teach catchers to never tag with the ball.

- Remind catchers to tag with the ball in the glove and the bare hand covering it. It will be much more difficult for the runner to knock the ball out of the catcher's mitt than out of the bare hand.

Pay Attention

- The catcher should be aware of any other baserunners who may try to advance during or after the play at the plate.

- The catcher should not argue with the umpire about whether he made the correct call. Too many times runners have advanced and

even scored while catchers are busy jawing at the ump about what they perceive to be a bad call.

- A catcher should keep his head in the game and let the coach worry about arguing.

INFIELD POSITIONING
Important for players of all ages

Learning what to do and when to do it is important for young infielders.

When younger players first start out playing the infield, it is often difficult for them to grasp the concept of where they should be playing. Sure, they know what the positions are and generally where they should be standing. But as a game evolves, many of them have no idea what to do when different situations arise.

There are some basic concepts that need to be laid out early if your team is going to have a good infield. Talk to each infielder and explain what their responsibilities are when they are fielding their position. Let the third baseman know what it means to guard the line, what it means to play at double play depth, or what it means to play off the base.

Then go around the infield as practice progresses and explain the roles of each player. Simulate game situations in

No Runners On

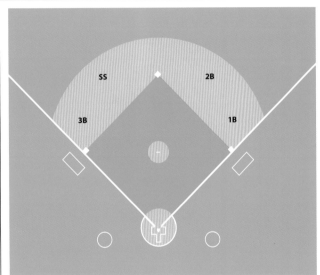

- When there are no runners on base, the infielders will play back in their normal positions.

- The shortstop and second baseman will be back, nearly touching the outfield grass.

- The first baseman will play back and off the line.

- The third baseman will also play off the line but might actually pinch in depending on the speed of the batter.

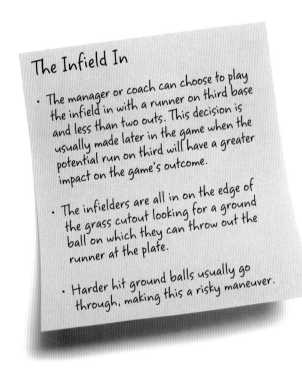

The Infield In

- The manager or coach can choose to play the infield in with a runner on third base and less than two outs. This decision is usually made later in the game when the potential run on third will have a greater impact on the game's outcome.

- The infielders are all in on the edge of the grass cutout looking for a ground ball on which they can throw out the runner at the plate.

- Harder hit ground balls usually go through, making this a risky maneuver.

practice so that the infielders can work on performing when there is only one strike on the hitter with a runner on first base or if there are runners at second and third with less than two outs in a tie game.

Your players, especially the younger ones, will not be aware of what to do right away. They have no point of reference and haven't spent enough time watching or playing the game to get a true feel for it.

You will find that the best way to enlighten them is through repetition. Have your outfielders and your bench players ready and on the bases. Hit grounders to the infielders without telling them where the ball is going. Bark out situations and see how they react when making a play. Praise them when they make the correct play and point out what they did wrong if they don't.

There are no etched-in-stone responses to every situation in a baseball game. But some are more accepted than others and these are the ones you need to work on with them.

Fewer than Two Strikes

- If there are fewer than two strikes and the batter is a threat to bunt, the third baseman should play a step or two in front of the base.

- If there are fewer than two strikes and the batter is not quick or a threat to bunt, the third baseman can play even with the base. This will still give him the opportunity to field a bunt.

Two Strikes

- If there are two strikes, the third baseman can return to his normal position a few steps behind the base.

- Unless the batter is an accomplished bunter and very quick, more often than not a bunt will not be attempted with two strikes for fear of striking out.

- The situation will also be dictated by how many men are on base or what the game situation is, but generally the third baseman will move back with two strikes.

OUTFIELD POSITIONING
Stay straight away and you will have a good day

It would be easy to say read the introduction to infield positioning and apply the same theories here. But there are differences when it comes to learning how to position the outfield and finding who is the best fit at each spot.

Determine who is your best and quickest defender, stick him in center field, and leave him there. A fast center fielder with a good glove can make up for many shortcomings among the corner outfielders, particularly at the younger levels. He can use his speed to cover much of the outfield, into the gaps, and even into where the left and right fielders play.

Try to find a right fielder that has a big, strong arm. His throws to the plate and third base are going to be longer than the ones made by the center and left fielder. Historically, some of the players with the greatest arms have played in right field, including Roberto Clemente, Dave Parker, and Carl Furillo. They can be a huge asset defensively in preventing

Straight Up

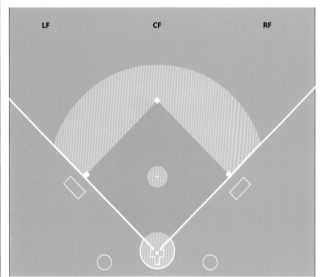

Be Ready

- Unless the coach or manager directs them otherwise, outfielders should always play "straight up."

- "Straight up" is when the left fielder plays almost directly behind the shortstop, the right fielder almost directly behind the second baseman, and the center fielder directly behind second base.

- Playing straight up will afford the outfielders their best chance to get to any balls that are hit in the gaps or in the corners.

- The infielders are always told to be in the ready position before each pitch, but the same rule applies to the outfielders.

- Players shouldn't get caught napping in the outfield. A player can go several innings without touching the ball and concentration can lapse, so he must pay attention to each and every pitch, preparing as if the ball will be hit to them.

- Outfielders should be ready to run.

the opposition from taking an extra base.

The left fielder doesn't need the biggest arm or to be the fleetest of foot. He simply needs to be stable, mobile enough to catch the ball, and know what to do once he has it.

YELLOW ● LIGHT

Some outfielders like to play very shallow in order to get to weakly hit ground balls quicker or be in a position to make a throw to the plate. It's also a good way to mask a weak throwing arm. If they are not fast, though, many fly balls will end up over their heads.

Think

- Part of getting ready for each pitch is thinking about what to do if the ball is hit your way.

- Teach outfielders to prepare for each possible scenario. What route will they take to the ball? To what base should it be thrown? Which way is the wind blowing? Are their sunglasses ready? These are just some of the questions to consider before every pitch is thrown.

Watch the Batter

- It sounds obvious, but teach players to watch to see whether or not the batter swings. If he begins to stride and swing, then there is a chance the ball will be hit their way.

- Also stress listening for the sound of the bat on the ball. When a ball is hit a certain way or for a certain distance, it makes a distinctive sound. Learning these sounds and how to move in response will allow an outfielder to become better defensively.

GENERAL FIELDING

CATCHING FLY BALLS

The rule of two applies—always use two hands when catching a fly ball

Preparing to catch a popup or fly ball is not difficult. It takes some thought, but otherwise it is one of the most basic plays in baseball, whether we're talking about infielders or outfielders. Simply track the ball, get under it, and catch it.

It sounds easy enough, but as a coach you need to make sure that your players are not hotdogging it when making a catch. Always insist that your players use two hands and position themselves properly. Never let them use one hand, or catch the ball off to the side or down by their waists. Snatch catching isn't acceptable either. That's when the fielder grabs the ball with one hand and snaps his wrist and hand down to his waist.

The Center Fielder

- Earlier we called the catcher the field general. The center fielder is one of his chief lieutenants.

- The center fielder is in charge of the outfield. Generally he is the quickest among the three and the best fielder.

- He has the authority to call off the right fielder or the left fielder when making a close play. He also has the authority to call off the second baseman or the shortstop when coming in to make a play behind second base.

Coming In

- The outfielder coming in to make a catch, regardless of position, should always call off the infielder.

- The outfielder has a better view of the ball and the infielders. He also has better balance running in than an infielder who is backpedaling, wondering whether he will run into the outfielder.

- The outfielder needs to be loud and let the infielder know he is charging in once he commits to making the catch.

This is Baseball 101. Teach your players early how to catch a fly ball properly and it is something that will stick with them their entire careers for however long they may last. If you allow them to get lazy when catching a popup or fly ball, then they will continue to be lazy in other aspects of the game and will only pick up more bad habits.

There is no room for discussion on this subject. Two hands must be used when catching a fly ball.

ZOOM

Hall of Famer Willie Mays popularized the basket catch in the 1950s and 1960s. He would get under a fly ball, place his glove at his waist, and let the ball fall into it like an apple falling from a tree. While flashy, it is not a recommended style for catching fly balls.

Square Up

- The outfielder should square his body up to the ball when making the catch, doing his best to keep the ball in front of him when possible.

- By keeping the ball in front of him, the outfielder puts himself in a better position to make a throw back to the infield should there be runners on base.

- The outfielder should be set under the ball. He should not be fidgety or move around.

The Hands

- The fielder should *always* use two hands when catching a fly ball.

- The glove hand should be up and the outfielder should be tracking the ball over the top of the glove.

- The fielder should keep the bare hand near the glove to squeeze it tight once the ball is caught.

- Having the throwing hand up and available near the glove also makes it easier to retrieve the ball and throw it back to the infield as opposed to the one-handed catch.

GENERAL FIELDING

ABOUT FIELDING GROUNDERS
Keep the glove down and stay in front of every ground ball

Unless you have players whose arms are 6 feet long, there will be some bending involved in fielding grounders. There's no getting around it. Sometimes, though, younger players tend to have a problem staying down on a ground ball. It can be frustrating when you have to remind them on play after play that they must get down in front of the ball. Very often they are impatient or do not realize that they need to have their gloves touching the ground in order to make some plays.

There isn't much that can be done other than practicing and reminding them that they have to stay down. Drill this point into them over and over again. After a while the concept should begin to sink in. Point out to them, in an encouraging manner, every time they pull up too soon on a grounder or don't get down in time on one.

Embarrassing moments when the ball goes between the fielder's legs can be avoided by simply staying down—and

KNACK COACHING YOUTH BASEBALL

Don't Wait

- There is no need for the infielder to wait for the ball. The infielder should take a step toward the ball and read the hop as it approaches.

- Be aggressive when fielding grounders. If the infielder

is tentative or undecided, then the chances of committing an error increase.

- Waiting for a grounder can make for an awkward play and cause the infielder to become unbalanced.

Don't Stand

- Players should field grounders in a crouched position, knees bent slightly.

- The infielder must keep his bottom down. If his bottom is up, then there's a good chance the ball will go under the glove.

- The player should look the ball into the glove and use the two-handed "crocodile" method of fielding it. This is when the free hand covers the glove in a manner that resembles a crocodile jaw after the ball has been fielded.

that means keeping that backside down and tucked in—and keeping the ball in front of them. It's nothing that a few hundred grounders in practice over the course of a season won't cure.

Don't Rush the Throw

- The infielder cannot throw the ball if he doesn't have possession of it, so there's no need to rush the throw.

- The player should concentrate on fielding the ball first. The infielder needs to make sure the ball is in the glove and that he has a firm grip on it with his throwing hand before attempting a throw.

- Too often an infielder will rush and begin throwing the ball before he has possession of it.

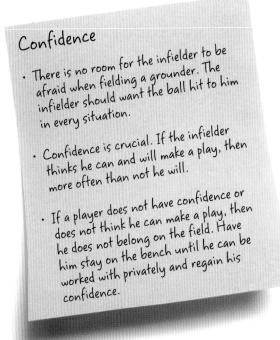

Confidence

- There is no room for the infielder to be afraid when fielding a grounder. The infielder should want the ball hit to him in every situation.

- Confidence is crucial. If the infielder thinks he can and will make a play, then more often than not he will.

- If a player does not have confidence or does not think he can make a play, then he does not belong on the field. Have him stay on the bench until he can be worked with privately and regain his confidence.

GENERAL FIELDING

BACKING UP THE PLAY
Everyone needs a little help on the field, so be prepared to provide it

In case we hadn't mentioned it already, baseball is a team game. With nine players on the field at one time, there is little room for individualism. A good team will be well schooled in the fundamentals and will work together to ensure those fundamentals are enacted.

Part of being on a good team and being a good teammate is knowing when and how to pick up one of your teammates when they have made a mistake. That's where backing up the play comes in. If a player is aware of what is going on around her, then backing up the play should be second nature.

For many young players, though, the thought of running to another part of the field, even if it is only a few steps, is a foreign one. Most young players are unable to grasp the significance of backing up a play or helping out a teammate. It's not that they are selfish or do not wish to help. Mainly, it's because the thinking is a bit too abstract. As the players

Catcher and Pitcher

- On a ground ball to the infield, if there are no runners on base, the catcher should run down the first base line with the runner and back up the throw to the first baseman. If the ball gets by the first baseman, the catcher will be in position to retrieve and throw the runner out should he attempt to advance a base.

- The pitcher must back up home plate and third base on throws from the outfield.

Outfielders

- Outfielders need to pay attention to every play, even those that seem like routine ground balls in the infield.

- An outfielder, particularly the right fielder and the left fielder, should be moving in to the infield on ground balls in case the infielder makes an error or is unable to make a play.

- If there are runners on base, this will help prevent those runners from advancing an extra base or scoring should the ball get through.

get older and more experienced, they will naturally slide from one spot on the field to another in order to help make a play.

When they are first starting out, however, they need a little help, a great deal of encouragement, and a patient coach to help bring it all together. Position your players on the field and point out to them how easy it would be for them to move behind another player to back up a play. Explain how it could prevent runs and keep runners from moving up a base, all while helping a teammate recover should he make an error. Go through some drills and physically walk with them to where they should be if they are backing up a teammate. After going through these drills for a while, quiz them on where they should be in different situations and see what they've learned.

The Steal

- When there is a runner on first base, the center fielder needs to be as aware of a potential steal as the infielders.

- When the runner stealing second breaks from first, the center fielder needs to take a step in. If the batter does not make contact with the ball, the center fielder should charge in and back up the play in the event the catcher makes a wild throw or the infielder cannot handle the throw, preventing the runner from taking an extra base.

Middle Infielders

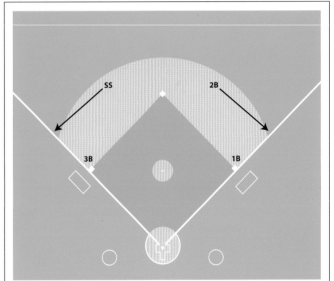

- Seldom will you see the middle infielders moving to back up the third baseman or first baseman.

- On what appear to be routine grounders to third or first, the shortstop and second baseman need to move at an angle behind the player fielding the ball in case of an error.

- If there is a runner advancing to third base, the shortstop should also be aware of the need to cover third base in the event of an error.

BE AGGRESSIVE

Remain aggressive: Give 100 percent on every play that comes your way and never take a play off

As is the case with any other sport or activity in which a child participates, confidence is essential. If a child is not confident in his abilities, the chances that he will be aggressive on the field of play are not good.

By aggressive, we do not mean violent; we do not mean getting physical with their teammates or the opposition.

Rather, the aggression of which we speak is directed toward their style of play. Be active and get involved in the play. Being passive on the field doesn't have any purpose.

Whether you are on the field or at the plate, waiting for something to happen rather than attacking the situation and making it happen can mean all the difference in the game. If

Errors

- The fielders, particularly the infielders, should stay with every play to its completion, even if they have made an error.

- The infielder does not know how slow or quick a runner is, so even if he boots the ball there is still a chance to make the play at first.

- Tell players to keep their heads up after making an error. Everyone makes errors and they should not be ashamed of it.

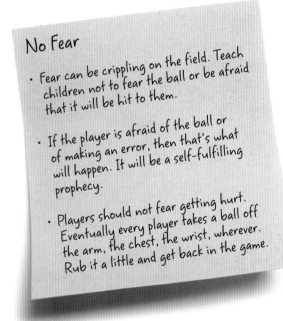

No Fear

- Fear can be crippling on the field. Teach children not to fear the ball or be afraid that it will be hit to them.

- If the player is afraid of the ball or of making an error, then that's what will happen. It will be a self-fulfilling prophecy.

- Players should not fear getting hurt. Eventually every player takes a ball off the arm, the chest, the wrist, wherever. Rub it a little and get back in the game.

a player sits with the bat on the shoulder and doesn't swing, then it is a wasted at-bat.

The same philosophy can be applied to playing the field. If a player sits back and waits for the ball to come to him or simply doesn't move after a ball because he lacks the confidence to make the play, then it is your responsibility as the coach to work with that player.

Build up their confidence and encourage them. Let them know that it's okay to make a mistake. Even the best players make mistakes. It is how they react to that mistake and what they learn from them that can make all the difference. So do not let your players act shy on the field. Have them attack the ball and go after it hard and fast. They must be proactive, not only to become better ballplayers but because they are part of a team and have others counting on them.

Wanting the Ball

- A player should hope that the ball gets hit to him. The player should want to make the play and want to be involved; otherwise there is no reason for him to be on the field.

- A fielder should cover as much ground as possible and go to great lengths to make a play. Baseball is supposed to be fun; go out and enjoy diving and sliding after every ball you can get to.

Encouragement

- Players should encourage their teammates after they make an error as they would want to be encouraged.

- Discourage ridicule, head shaking, or negative gestures that make players feel worse than they already feel.

- Ask players to give their teammates the same treatment they would want if they made the error themselves.

POSITIONING
Positioning and footwork are essential for first basemen

The first baseman, aside from the catcher, may have the most important job on the field. While the catcher is physically involved in every play of the game in one form or another, the first baseman is involved in one way or another in almost as many plays. The difference is that the catcher will be in the same position, save for moving a few inches, on every pitch. The first baseman, however, has to learn where and how to be positioned in order to be ready to make a play.

We've already noted that the catcher is the field general and usually a pretty smart player. The first baseman is akin to the catcher in that regard. As a coach, you need someone with a high baseball IQ who has the savvy to know when and how to move into position to make a play.

This isn't like playing third base or the other infield positions. First base requires much more thinking and involvement than the other positions, and that means knowing

Play Back

- The first baseman should be positioned a few steps behind the base if there are no runners on base.

- When taking up position, the first baseman should also be a few feet off the line to afford more of a chance to get to a ground ball in the hole between first and second base.

- The first baseman should know who is batting, though. If he has knowledge of where the batter usually hits the ball, he can make slight adjustments accordingly.

A Runner on First

- If there is a runner on first, depending on who the runner is, the first baseman should be positioned at the base, ready to accept the pickoff throw.

- While the first baseman needs to be ready to receive a pickoff throw, he can't ignore the fact that the batter may be preparing to bunt.

- The first baseman needs to be prepared to move forward for a bunt or move backward to his normal position should the batter swing away.

where to stand prior to every pitch. Other position players can get away with little positional mistakes. The first baseman cannot. He needs to be quick, agile, and ready to move in any direction before a pitch is even thrown.

A Slow Runner

- Knowledge of who is on base is helpful here.

- If the runner is slow, not a threat to steal, or not a threat to get a good jump, then the first baseman should play a step or two behind the runner and off the base.

- The first baseman should be patient when fielding a grounder hit his way if the runner is slow. Chances are, if there are fewer than two outs, he can make a force play at second base.

Move

- Under normal circumstances, when the ball is hit and it is not to the first baseman, he needs to move to first base. This should be second nature.

- The first baseman can't get caught napping when the ball is hit. He must be aware of where the ball is hit at all times.

- If the ball is hit on the ground, he needs to move to the base and accept the throw.

RECEIVING THE THROW
Players must be prepared to move any and all ways to catch a throw

Receiving a throw, especially for a younger first baseman, can be a scary thing. The body is stretched out and in a vulnerable position, there is a runner bearing down on first base, and there is a throw, hopefully a good one, being rifled somewhere in the general direction of the base.

There is a great deal going on, and the first baseman must focus on receiving the throw. Some first basemen are naturals at playing the position. They glide to the base, take a throw,

and get rid of the ball all in a fluid manner, never once showing any trepidation. Not every first baseman is a natural, though, and that is something as a coach that you need to anticipate.

Younger players in particular can look lost when learning how to play the position. As a result, this is one position in which a great deal of practice time is needed. The first baseman needs to be able to catch the ball, even if she is shaky while doing it. Start off slow, throwing easy balls across the

The Foot

- The first baseman must be aware of where her foot is in relationship to the base before accepting the throw.

- If the first baseman is right-handed, she should place her right foot against the base, not on it, and stretch with her glove hand, and

vice versa if she is left-handed.

- The foot should not be directly on the base because the runner can step on it and both players can sustain serious injury.

The Stretch

- Once the first baseman has placed his foot alongside the base, he can begin to prepare to accept the throw.

- The first baseman should wait as long as possible before going into the stretch. If the play won't be close at first, he can simply

take a step toward whichever fielder is throwing the ball without stretching.

- He should work on maintaining balance in the stretch. If the first baseman extends his front foot too far, he can topple or suffer an injury.

infield from every position. Make it so the first baseman can catch the ball and get a sense of what it looks like coming from various positions on the diamond.

This will help build up the first baseman's confidence. As she gets used to accepting a throw, start making them a little more difficult. Bounce them in at first; throw them a little high or a little wide. The first baseman has to know that she can and must move off the base to catch some throws. You can't have a first baseman that does not have the instincts to move to a ball or anticipate where it will be thrown.

The Bad Throw

- The first baseman should not be afraid to move to get the ball. He should stay on the base and move his arm accordingly to catch a throw as any other position player would.

- He should not, however, try and stretch 20 feet to catch a ball. The first baseman should move off the base to catch an errant throw even if it means the runner will be safe. It's better to step off and make the catch than let the ball get by.

Stay in Front

- The biggest objective for the first baseman, if the ball cannot be caught, is to stay in front of it.

- If the ball gets by the first baseman, the runners can and usually will advance. This can be costly.

- The first baseman can drop down to one knee or smother the ball in any way possible to keep it from going to the fence or into the dugout or stands.

HOLDING THE RUNNER

Keeping the runner close at first base can prevent a big inning by the opposition

Much of the responsibility of holding the runner on first base will fall on the pitcher. If he throws over often enough, the runner will be less inclined to run. If he is quick to the plate with his pitches, the runner will be less inclined to run. The onus, however, isn't solely on the pitcher.

The first baseman has a job to do here as well and that

means more than just catching the ball. Let's start there, though. The first baseman needs to be able to catch the ball and slap a tag on the runner all in one motion. This requires good instincts and quick reflexes. Making a tag on a pickoff play is a bang-bang action. There is no time to think, and very often the first baseman is simply slapping a tag into where

Foot Placement

- Whether the first baseman is right-handed or left-handed, the inside of the right foot should be placed flush along the inside edge of the base (the side of the base facing home plate).

- First basemen should avoid getting caught flat-footed or leaning back against the

base. It can be disruptive to the footwork and cause loss of balance.

- Rather, the right foot goes alongside the base as a guide and the left foot steps toward the pitcher.

The Target

- The first baseman needs to set a target, similar to what a catcher would do when setting up for a pitch.

- The first baseman should make sure the target is

steady. The pitcher is making a quick look and a quick throw over to first, an action that is much more difficult to perform if he does not have an idea where he is throwing the ball.

124

he thinks the runner will be because he has no time to turn and see where the runner actually is.

Some pitchers and their first basemen have a good chemistry. Some even work out little signals to indicate that a throw is coming. This isn't a bad idea because it would be a shame if the first baseman were caught off guard or surprised that the pitcher actually wheeled around and fired a throw to first. That can lead to a throwing error and a runner winding up on third base.

Ideally, the first baseman you choose will be left-handed.

It is much easier for a left-handed first baseman to apply a tag on a pickoff play because he simply has to drop the glove down in most cases rather than drag it across the body. Right-handed first basemen aren't uncommon and some are very good at playing the position. Try to look for a lefty however, because it will make your job a bit easier.

Glove Positioning

- The first baseman should hold the glove so the pitcher can clearly distinguish it from his body and the background.

- Players should wait for the ball and avoid stabbing or lunging for the ball unless it is a bad throw.

- Keeping the glove steady when receiving the throw will make it easier to just bring the hand down and apply the tag rather than swinging it back into the runner.

Be Ready to Move

- The first baseman needs to be prepared to make a move after it has been determined whether the pitcher will throw to him or go to the plate with a pitch.

- If the pitcher goes to the plate, the first baseman needs to jump back into

the play and be prepared to field a ball or receive a throw from another infielder.

- He should be prepared to throw to second in the event the runner has been picked off.

THE BALL IN THE HOLE

The ability to go to the right is an integral part of a first baseman's repertoire

Not every first baseman is gifted enough athletically to move to his right fluidly when fielding a ground ball. The play is tough enough for an average player, but if the player is clumsy, does not have good footwork, or looks more like a tree toppling over rather than someone diving for the ball, then some work is in order.

In most instances, the first baseman won't have to be guarding the line, particularly early in the game. This will give him a bit of an edge when it comes to fielding the ball in the hole between first and second base. He can cheat off the line and take a few steps toward the second baseman so he can get to any balls hit in the hole a little quicker.

Making a Commitment

- There is no room for indecision when making the play in the hole between first and second base. The first baseman needs to decide whether he will or won't play the ball the moment it is hit.

- If the first baseman is wishy-washy or undecided, then he will be prone to committing an error or making no play at all.

- He should not assume the second baseman will make the play if the ball gets through.

The Race Is On

- Once the first baseman has decided to go after the ball and actually makes the play, it is time for another decision—race to the base or toss the ball to the pitcher, who should be covering.

- If the first baseman decides he can catch the runner on his own, he must signal to the pitcher as both players sprint toward first. If the pitcher is watching the first baseman, he will back off the play.

Work with your first baseman on this. You obviously can't teach speed, but if you hit your first baseman enough grounders and have him practice moving to his right often enough, his play will improve. But that is only half of it. You, as a coach, have homework to do while also relying on your observation skills.

Know who the opposition is and what their tendencies are at the plate. Know which right-handed batters will go the other way on the ground and which left-handed hitters will pull the ball. Watch every at-bat carefully so you can properly position your players the second time through the opposition's batting order.

You will never make a first baseman that isn't fleet of foot fast. But you can improve his quickness by helping him out through practice and teaching him the benefits of observation and knowing the opposition. Some hard work and a little knowledge can go a long way in making an average first baseman a good one.

The Lead

- If the first baseman decides the runner will beat him to the bag, then he must get the ball to the pitcher quickly.

- The first baseman should lead the pitcher with a soft toss, one that will be in front of the pitcher and arrive at the base the same time he does.

- If the first baseman throws the ball too hard or too far, the pitcher will not be able to reach it, resulting in an error.

Communicate

- If there are runners on base, particularly a runner heading from second to third on the play, it is essential for the first baseman to communicate with the pitcher.

- Because the pitcher will be running toward first base, facing the right field line, he will have his back to the infield and not be able to see any advancing runners.

- It is the first baseman's job to let the pitcher know if the runner on second or third is advancing.

FIELDING THE BUNT
Players should be aggressive without being reckless when fielding a bunt

A first baseman that can take charge on a sacrifice and field a bunt cleanly and quickly can be a game-changing player. She can cut down a lead runner, take away scoring chances, and stem the tide of a rally if she has the ability and the know-how to field a bunt and get rid of it quickly.

These are particularly good traits to have when playing youth baseball simply because many of the games center on moving runners from station to station. If a coach is a good one, then he is stressing fundamentals, and part of solid, fundamental baseball is being able to move a runner over via the bunt. So, as a good coach yourself, you must be able to counter the opposition and prepare for the bunt in the best way possible.

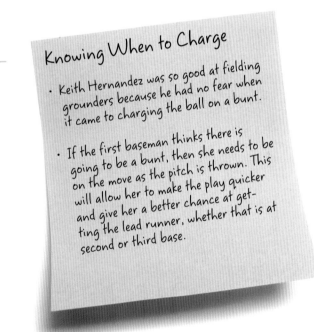

Knowing When to Charge

- Keith Hernandez was so good at fielding grounders because he had no fear when it came to charging the ball on a bunt.

- If the first baseman thinks there is going to be a bunt, then she needs to be on the move as the pitch is thrown. This will allow her to make the play quicker and give her a better chance at getting the lead runner, whether that is at second or third base.

Two Hands

- Unless the ball is at a complete stop, the first baseman should use two hands to field it.

- There is less of a chance that the first baseman will commit an error if he is scooping the ball into the glove with his free hand.

- Once the first baseman has fielded the ball he must check the runners, including the batter, and decide which base he will go to with the ball.

This is an easy part of the game to practice because your team also needs to practice bunting. So when you are working on your bunting drills, don't just use them as filler at the beginning or end of batting practice. Use the time wisely and have the infielders work on handling the bunt while the rest of your team works on improving its bunting skills.

ZOOM

We mentioned Keith Hernandez earlier in this chapter and with good reason. The Gold Glove first baseman would routinely field bunts on the *third base* side of the mound, because his instincts and talent level were that great. Not every first baseman will be able to do this, but one with vision could make it happen occasionally.

Listen

Confidence

- If the first baseman has committed to fielding the ball, then he must be ready to listen.

- If the catcher and the pitcher have been instructed properly, they will be screaming out to the first baseman about which base he should be throwing the ball.

- While there is generally a great deal of confusion, the first baseman must keep a clear head and listen to the direction of his teammates.

- Thinking there is going to be a bunt and having the confidence to do anything about it are two different things.

- A good fielder, regardless of the position, will never shy away from making a play.

The first baseman needs to have confidence when fielding the bunt.

- A lack of confidence will lead to indecision, a poor throw, or making a fielding error.

THROWING TO SECOND
The ability to make a strong, accurate throw to second base is key

When a runner is on first base, the first baseman needs to be thinking about what she will be doing with the ball if it is hit to her. While this should be standard practice before any play any player makes, it is particularly important for a first baseman to be aware of where she will be going with the ball because a great deal hinges on her actions.

If she elects to go to second in an attempt to get the lead runner and is too slow in making the play, the opposition will have two runners on base, including one in scoring position. If she makes an error or makes a poor throw going to second, the runner could end up on third base with the batter possibly reaching second.

The first baseman can also go to first base with the play and simply ignore the runner, but then the opposition will have a runner in scoring position. So many choices and so little time to make a decision. That's why it's important for

Be Aggressive
- While good judgment is always of paramount importance, the better first basemen will usually approach the play aggressively and try to throw to second under almost any circumstances.

- Aggression does not replace common sense, i.e., if there is no one covering the base or it is clear the runner will be safe, the player should turn and make the play at first base.

Throwing

- A left-handed first baseman will have an easier time than a right-handed first baseman when throwing to second because he does not have to turn his body to do so.

- This play becomes a bit easier if the first baseman is running toward second base to field the ball. His momentum will carry him toward the base, and often he will be even or ahead of the runner, making the throw that much easier.

you as the coach to impress upon your first baseman the importance of thinking before each play when there are runners on base.

There will be many times that despite having a well-thought-out plan, mistakes happen or the runner will be safe anyway. But those instances are fewer and farther between when there is a plan of action in place before the play takes place. So decide what your philosophy will be on the subject and impart that knowledge to your players.

Making the throw to second base can be a very difficult play. But if a first baseman is well prepared, the chances of her making a mistake will decrease considerably.

Judgment

- Knowing when to make the throw to second base is important.

- When the first baseman fields the ball after going into the hole, he must have a clear sight line to second base. If the runner from first is blocking his view of the base or the player covering the base, it would be wise to not attempt a throw.

- A throw can be made with a little help from the shortstop, who should offer guidance.

The Pivot

- The right-handed first baseman will have to worry about making the pivot when he throws.

- If he has fielded the ball in front of the runner or on the grass, the first baseman must quickly spin his body around on his right foot (the pivot) and set up to throw to second base.

- The jump pivot, much like the one a middle infielder makes when turning a double play, is also effective when going for balls behind the runner.

PREPARING TO PLAY
A little pregame knowledge and preparation never hurts

Second base isn't the glamour position in the infield. It doesn't have a nickname like the hot corner, it doesn't have the cache that shortstop has, and it isn't nearly as involved as playing first base. Yet, for many, second base remains the glue in the infield, holding it together.

Before a second baseman is able to hold an infield together, though, he has to be prepared to take the field himself. His own house must be in order before he can help bring a much larger gathering together. As a coach, there are certain things that you can do to expedite this process, but much of the prep work has to be done by the player himself.

Finding the right glove is something that a youngster won't be able to do on his own. Traditionally, this is a parent's job, but you may find that some of your players don't have a parent who is up to the task. You may need to step in and help. Show your player what the right glove and the wrong glove

Before Taking the Field

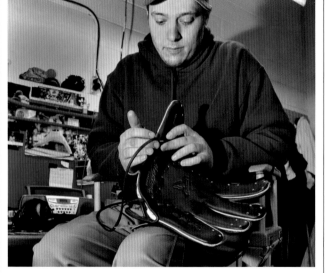

- It is important that the second baseman have the proper glove to play the position.

- A smaller glove, one of the smallest on the field, is better than a larger one. The ball can get lost in a larger glove, which is something

- an infielder never wants to happen.

- It is easier to retrieve a ball from a smaller glove.

- A smaller glove is more manageable when moving laterally.

Only One Glove

- Despite the trend among professionals, youngsters should not use a batting glove underneath the glove.

- A batting glove can impact the feel a regular glove provides, especially if the

- regular glove is still stiff and not completely broken in.

- Younger players, more so than older ones, need to be able to feel the ball in their gloves as much as they need to see it.

look and feel like and let him make a decision from there on what feels comfortable.

Much of the rest lies with the player. He needs to get accustomed to his glove. You can't do that for him. He also needs to become familiar with his position. You can walk him out to second base and explain the nuances of the position to him, but your experience of standing in the infield won't mirror his. This is something he needs to learn on his own and in his own way.

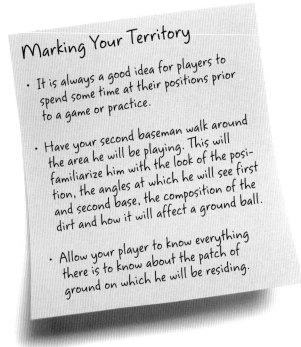

Marking Your Territory

- It is always a good idea for players to spend some time at their positions prior to a game or practice.

- Have your second baseman walk around the area he will be playing. This will familiarize him with the look of the position, the angles at which he will see first and second base, the composition of the dirt and how it will affect a ground ball.

- Allow your player to know everything there is to know about the patch of ground on which he will be residing.

Your Glove

- Your players need to think of their gloves as extensions of their hands. This is particularly true of the second baseman.

- The player should work the glove, oil it, pound it, make it so that it molds to the hand and fits, well, like a glove.

- Stress that the glove should be treated with respect. It is the tool an infielder needs to succeed, and a good glove is one that a player can use for years.

133

TIME TO PLAY
Get ready for the ball to be put in play

When coaching children, especially younger children, one of the most difficult tasks a coach has is getting her players to focus. There is a great deal of down or wasted time in youth baseball as pitchers struggle to find the plate. Younger hitters often struggle as well in coach-pitch leagues.

This all leads to too much dead time in between pitches, which leads to playing with the dirt, daydreaming, or simply not paying attention. It can't be stressed enough that you must encourage your players to focus for each and every pitch, particularly those playing the infield. Help them find a pre-pitch routine and have them stick with it pitch after pitch until it becomes second nature.

Not only will having this pre-pitch routine give the players something to do in between pitches, it will help keep them focused. Invariably it is when a player is not focused that the ball will find him. How many times do you see a grounder

Be Aware

- The second baseman gets into the ready position, with his hands on his knees, which are slightly bent.

- The second baseman has a great deal of ground to cover on either side and through the middle of the

diamond. He needs to be prepared to move quickly in either direction or into the outfield to make a play.

- He should be cognizant of where the other infielders are positioned to avoid confusion or collisions.

The Pitcher

- The second baseman should keep an eye on the pitcher.

- When the pitcher begins his delivery, this means the ball will be put into play and the second baseman should be ready to spring into action.

- The second baseman has a particular advantage if a left-handed pitcher is on the mound because he can follow the entire flight of the ball and know exactly where it is. He can lose sight of it for a second if a right-hander is on the mound.

slide by an infielder because the infielder was busy playing with his hat, talking to another player, or simply staring at the ground?

If you want your players to be sharp and fundamentally sound, then the best bet is to have them develop a pre-pitch routine. Work on this with them. Have them take the same steps each time by getting into the ready position, watching the pitcher, knowing what the count is, etc. Repetition is a wonderful reinforcement tool.

For a second baseman, this would include arranging the other infielders, checking with the shortstop on who will cover second if there is a man on first, and keeping a close on the pitcher when there are runners on base. Pitchers will often signal when there will be a pickoff attempt, and the second baseman will be affected by any pickoff attempts involving runners on first or second base. So urge your players to stay sharp.

Use Your Head

- One of the biggest challenges for a young player is learning how to think ahead.

- Stress over and over again to your players that they must think about what they are going to do if the ball is hit to them.

- Run through scenarios with them, particularly second basemen who are involved with double plays and could be required to cover or back up two bases.

Moving Time

- Once the ball is pitched, players bring their hands off their knees and crouch over just a bit more, letting their hands swing free in front.

- The arms need to be prepared and ready to field a grounder, not swinging wildly and uncontrolled.

- Second basemen must shift the weight to the balls of the feet and be ready to move laterally in order to reach a grounder, line drive, or popup.

135

FIELDING THE GROUNDER
Practice really does make perfect when talking about ground balls

Fielding a grounder is an easy task. Or so everyone would lead you to believe. For youngsters, though, panic can set in when the ball is hit their way. Indecision can flood their minds about what to do with the ball when they catch it. That's assuming they will catch it. The fear of making an error and looking foolish in front of friends and teammates can take something as simple as fielding a grounder and turn it into a stressful act.

So how do you combat that? For starters, keep the kids calm, assure them that everyone makes mistakes—errors are part of the game— and that no one will be finger-pointing or name-calling if they do make an error.

Hit them lots of grounders. Repetition is one of the best teachers. Also, encourage them when they make a mistake. They need to know that you aren't mad, and being able to trust you will go a long way toward relieving some of the

Stay Loose

- Young players tend to panic if the ball is hit toward them. Remind your infielders to stay loose and not stiffen up when a ball is hit their way.

- Second basemen, particularly if the ball is hit slowly,

can take a step forward and begin lowering their gloves when it becomes obvious they have a play.

- If your player is stiff or anxious, it will be more difficult to bend over and make a play.

Actual Fielding

- Players begin by bending over and rolling the glove hand downward so that the fingers and the ground are at a forty-five-degree angle.

- The glove should be open and ready to receive the ball.

- Teach the use of two hands whenever possible, closing the glove tightly around the ball once it has been fielded.

- The bare hand should be near the glove, ready to snatch the ball out and begin the throwing process.

stress associated with learning how to field a grounder.

As for the teaching, that part is simple. Use the crocodile method where the player employs two hands and closes his bare hand over the glove once he has fielded the ball, imitating a crocodile's jaw snapping shut. Do not encourage or allow hotdogging it when it comes to fielding.

There should be no grabbing the ball on the side of the body with one hand. Instruct your players to get in front of the ball as often as possible and use two hands to field it. There is a greater chance of making an error when using only one hand or when trying to show off. Tell them that making the play properly and not getting charged with an error is the best way to show off and let their teammates know how good of a fielder they are.

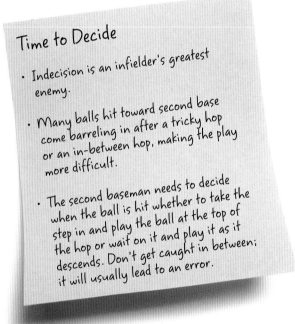

Time to Decide

- Indecision is an infielder's greatest enemy.

- Many balls hit toward second base come barreling in after a tricky hop or an in-between hop, making the play more difficult.

- The second baseman needs to decide when the ball is hit whether to take the step in and play the ball at the top of the hop or wait on it and play it as it descends. Don't get caught in between; it will usually lead to an error.

Watch It

- The old adage is that a player should look the ball into his glove. It is not just a saying; it is a sound piece of advice.

- If the second baseman is busy looking toward first, watching the runner, or fretting about making a throw, the ball will never find its way into the glove.

- Players should make sure the ball is securely in the glove before standing upright and attempting a throw.

MAKING THE THROW
Making the throw to first is more difficult than it seems

The throw from where the second baseman is normally positioned to first base is the easiest of the three infield throws. It does not require the cannon that a shortstop must possess to make a throw from deep in the hole, nor does it require the urgency that many throws from third base do.

That said, the throw made by a second baseman should not be overlooked or considered a given. It is simply an easier throw to make than the aforementioned tosses. Therefore,

the second baseman and the first baseman should still practice working on the throw. It takes time to develop a fundamentally sound throwing pattern. The more time and preparation work a player puts in, the less likely he is to commit a throwing error.

The best way to work on throws to first base is to do a little extra infield practice before or after the team meets for its regularly scheduled practice. Break out the fungo bat and hit

You Have Time

- Players should not rush the throw. More often than not, especially when playing second base, there is time to set and make a proper throw.

- The second baseman should think of it as simply playing catch with the first baseman. This will result in a nice, easy, manageable throw.

- As the second baseman makes this throw more and more, it will become second nature. At that point, much of the angst involved should disappear.

Overhand

- It is very important for players to remember to throw the ball overhand.

- Tell your players: *Do not* sidearm the ball and *do not* throw it three-quarters.

- Players should throw the ball like it was meant to be thrown, like they are trying to reach the first baseman. A weak throw can come up short and lead to an error, while a sidearm/three-quarter throw can go wide and pull the first baseman or shortstop off the base.

a few dozen grounders to your second baseman and have him throw over to first. Some youngsters are very eager and receptive to the extra work and will push you for more time on the field. If that turns out to be the case with your second baseman, then bravo, you have a ballplayer on your hands.

ZOOM

Having trouble throwing to first base is often referred to as 'the yips.' Former Yankees second baseman Chuck Knoblauch was a four-time All-Star and a Gold Glove winner whose career began to slide downhill when he developed a case of the yips. He committed twenty-six errors in 1999, two years after winning the Gold Glove.

Underhanded

- There are certain instances when an overhand throw isn't necessary.

- If the player is moving toward second base or is close to the bag, an underhand toss may be more convenient or effective depending on the proximity to the base or the position of the body.

- Put a little mustard on the underhand throw, but not so much that the recipient can't catch the ball.

Don't Panic

- Players often panic when faced with making a throw.

- Throwing the baseball is the most natural part of the game. Teach players to find the person to whom they are throwing and let it go.

- Players should block out everything else around them, whether it is runners on base or the batter heading to first.

COVERING THE BASE

It is important to know who is covering the base in every situation

There is always a buzz of activity in the middle infield. The shortstop and the second baseman are among the game's most active players, and since they work in concert so often, they must be able to communicate effectively and freely in order to determine who will be covering the base on a given play.

When looking for middle infielders on your team, it is always a good idea to have players who are friendly or at the very

least familiar with one another. Younger players sometimes have a tougher time adapting to playing with someone they do not like and as a result, there are the occasional communication breakdowns.

Such problems can lead to second base going uncovered or worse, a player trying to cover the base himself without taking advantage of having a teammate in the vicinity. It is imperative that you stress the fact that the base needs to be

Communication

- Talking to the shortstop is important.

- The second baseman needs to communicate with the shortstop about who will be covering the base on attempted steals and certain ground balls in the infield.

- While the communication can be verbal, it is often done through hand signals or gestures in order to prevent the opposing team from knowing who will be covering the base.

The Straddle

- Learning how to cover the base on an attempted steal is essential.

- Players place the left foot on the side of the base that faces first base and the right foot on the side that faces third base so the point of the base is almost sticking out between the two feet.

- The left foot will provide somewhat of an impediment to a runner attempting to slide into the base.

covered and that the shortstop and the second baseman need to work together.

Have your middle infielders work closely together and become familiar with one another so that ultimately there is no need to worry about whether the base will be covered. Eventually, if they hit it off, the duo will develop their own system on how to communicate and how to make sure all areas of the middle infield are accounted for.

A good middle infield tandem can read each other's thoughts and actions, and when that happens it is a beautiful thing to watch. The symmetry and grace of a well-oiled middle infield is a treat for any coach, but when you can forge such a grouping at a younger age, it is even more impressive.

Send your second baseman and shortstop out on their own before or after practice and let them work through getting to know each other's habits and idiosyncrasies. The benefits will be well worth the time they put in.

Movement

- A second baseman must be prepared to move if there is a runner on first base.

- When the ball is hit to the left side of the infield— either to the shortstop or the third baseman—the second baseman must break to the base.

- It is the second baseman's responsibility to take the throw from the left side of the infield to complete the force play or begin the double play.

Fear Factor

- Players must learn not be afraid of the runner.

- The split-second timing of making a catch and slapping down a tag while knowing a runner is bearing down can be stressful.

- Players should not worry what the runner is doing.

The infielder's first priority is to make the catch. If the catch isn't made, worrying about the tag is academic.

- A minor collision may ensue at the base. The infielder should brace himself in the event the runner slides forcefully.

141

THE DOUBLE PLAY

The twin killing is a pitcher's best friend and the fastest way to end an inning

A perfectly executed double play is a beautiful thing to watch. Whether it is a 6-4-3 twin killing or the 5-4-3 variety, it can squash a rally, boost a team, inspire the crowd, or simply give the players a chance to show off the fundamentals they have likely been practicing.

The key word in that sentence is practicing. A well-turned double play is an art form, one that does not come about simply because two players are in position to make the play. The double play is one act that requires a great deal of practice time to perfect, particularly if one of the participants isn't as gifted as the other or if neither has a handle on how to perform the task.

Concentration

- More so than just about any other throw a player receives, the initial catch a second baseman (or shortstop) makes in the double play process requires concentration.

- Players must concentrate: The rest of the play will not matter if the player covering second base does not catch the ball.

- Players should use two hands and make sure the ball is in the glove before attempting to throw to first.

The Lead

- This play is similar to the one a first baseman makes when leading a pitcher on a throw.

- Teach players to make sure the ball is not thrown too hard or it will beat the shortstop to the base. Conversely, an underthrown ball can pull the shortstop off the base and into the oncoming runner.

- The throw should always be chest high so the player covering the base doesn't have to reach for it.

The second baseman has the greater challenge when turning the double play because his back is to the runner. When the shortstop is on the pivot end of the double play, he is usually coming across the base and has the runner in front of him so he knows what to expect. The second baseman does not have that luxury. As a result, he has to trust his instincts, show a bit more courage, and block out the fact the runner may slide into him or over him and possibly cause an injury.

That is why it is important when looking for a second baseman among your players to find one who is tough enough to take a hit. It will take some work for the younger players to master the jump pivot or get out of the way of an oncoming runner. They will get hit early on and that may cause a few bumps and bruises and perhaps even a few tears.

So, find one of the grittier players on your team, explain to him why you chose him to play second base, and let him know what to expect when he takes the field.

The Pivot

- The second baseman should step on the base with his right foot as he is catching the ball.

- After catching the ball, the player steps forward with his left foot and makes the throw to first base.

- If the runner is sliding and there isn't time to move across the base in the aforementioned fashion, employ the jump pivot.

- The second baseman's left foot should be on the base as he catches the ball. While catching it, he should jump, pivot, and throw to avoid the sliding runner.

The Underhand Toss

- Receiving and throwing the underhand toss takes perfect timing.

- Players should keep the knees bent and the wrist locked, ensuring the ball will be tossed firmly but not too firmly.

- This can be practiced either on the bases in actual game-simulated situations or in the outfield by positioning several players in lines across from one another. In this drill, have the players step and toss, step and toss.

GETTING READY

It is important to go over some basics before heading out to play third base

A coach should always have his players prepared to play any position. That should go without saying, but sometimes even the best coaches need a gentle reminder about getting their players ready. The reminder about getting their players ready to play third base is not going to be so gentle, though.

Third base is a very difficult position to play, and there is as much responsibility on the coach as there is on the player when it comes to being prepared. The speed of a game is much different than the speed of what takes place in practice. So while you, as a coach, can hit grounder after grounder out to your third baseman and drill him on what to do with it, simulating the adrenaline rush and speed of a game is tough to match.

Expectations

- Third basemen must be ready for anything at any time; it can be the most dangerous position on the field.

- Balls come off the bat much quicker for the third baseman and the reaction time is much shorter than that of the second baseman and shortstop.

- The other infielders, while not advisable, can take their eye off the batter for a split second. Third basemen don't have that luxury because of the speed at which the ball can reach them.

Talking

- Third basemen need to talk with their middle infielders, either verbally or through hand signals, when runners are on base.

- The third baseman does this so he knows who will be covering the base and what to expect should he

- opt to make a throw to second base.

- He also needs to communicate with his pitcher about what to do and expect should there be a bunt on the third base side of the mound.

Because that is the case, talk to your third baseman. Let him know what it will be like in a game. Eventually experience will be his best teacher and he will learn how to handle the rigors of the position. Initially, though, it is imperative that you make him aware of what to expect. Don't try to scare him. That's not your objective. Simply prepare him for what to expect once he takes the field for the first time under game conditions.

Popups

- The third baseman needs to be vocal and take charge on an infield popup on his side of the mound and in foul territory.

- A popup near the dugout is the third baseman's ball. He should call off the catcher because he is running into the ball and has a better view of the dugout and the railing.

- The third baseman should call off the pitcher and the catcher when the popup is between the mound and the third base foul line.

You Gotta Think

- Because the reaction time is so quick at third base, the person playing the position needs to have his thinking cap on.

- Before every pitch, the third baseman needs to think about what he is going to do with the ball if it is hit to him, particularly if there are runners on base.

- This will eliminate any panic or indecision that may arise when and if the ball is actually hit his way.

ATTITUDE

How players approach playing third base is as important as their actual performance on the field

Third basemen have an edge to them. It comes with the territory.

This is such a tough position to play that it takes a special kind of player, not only one who wants to be out there but one who expects to be abused at any given moment. The abuse of which we speak is not verbal or from another person. Rather, it is from the baseball and the position itself.

Catchers get beat up—that is a given. But so do third basemen. The distance between the third baseman and home plate is often less than 90 feet—should the third baseman be playing in on the grass—and when the ball rockets off the bat, there is precious little time to make a decision.

Getting Hurt

- If you have a player who is afraid of the ball or of getting hurt, then he shouldn't be playing third base.

- Third base is a position that requires a fearless approach. If your third baseman has any hesita-tion or trepidation, then he probably should not be playing the position.

- This is a position that should be played by someone who is tough both mentally and physically.

Getting Hit

- Next to the catcher, the third baseman might be the most bruised and banged up player on the field.

- No matter how good of a fielder the third baseman is, because the ball comes at him with such speed, he invariably takes his share of hard hops off his chest and arms. This means bruises, aches, and pains are commonplace. The good third baseman will expect them and become immune to them.

It is called the hot corner for a reason. The ball is hit so hard and so fast that it can "scorch" the person playing the position, hence the nickname. It takes a special breed of player to excel at third base. Consider there are fewer third basemen than any other position in the Hall of Fame and that will give you an idea of what it takes to achieve true greatness at the position.

So as a coach, take your time when choosing who will play the hot corner for you. It is a position that truly needs some nurturing and some patience, because very few youngsters will be able to step in and adapt quickly to the speed as well as the rough and tumble nature of playing third base.

Find one of the tougher kids on the team, one who doesn't bruise so easily, either physically or mentally. Work with him, explaining what the position entails, what to expect, and how much of a challenge it really is.

Welcoming the Challenge

- Third base is not for the faint of heart. It is a position in which a gauntlet is thrown down before the person who plays it.

- The third baseman should welcome the challenge of playing the position and view it as a game within the game.

- The third baseman needs to be eager to prove himself on every play and look for the ball to be hit his way.

Be a Leader

- We have already acknowledged the catcher as a natural team leader, but because of the nature of third base, the person who plays this position is usually also a team leader.

- Many third basemen are vocal, take charge in the infield, and counsel the pitcher when he finds himself in trouble.

- Because a third baseman is expected to be tougher, he has to lead by example.

147

RUNNERS ON BASE

It is time to make a quick decision when there are runners on the move

The fast decision-making process involved with playing third base only gets more complicated when there are runners on base. Now, aside from having to be ready to act quickly, a third baseman has to be ready to decide what to do with the ball should it come to her and then execute the play properly. Oh, and this all takes place in an instant.

This process requires a third baseman that is surehanded and decisive. If there are runners on base and the third baseman is jittery or prone to bobbling the ball, then it will only benefit the opposition. You want someone who is authoritative and not afraid to take action manning the hot corner in these situations.

Going Home

- When the bases are loaded, the first play on a grounder to third is to go home with it and get the force play if there are less than two outs.

- If there are two outs, the third baseman should simply step on third to end the inning. Throwing to first

or second is also an option if there is no time to reach third base.

- These plays can be difficult if the infield is in. The ball will get to the third baseman faster and will be more difficult to handle, so he should be prepared.

A Tricky One

- If there are fewer than two outs and the bases are loaded, the third baseman needs to be ready for a difficult double play.

- He should field the grounder, step on third, and

throw home in time to get the runner. It becomes a tag play at the plate rather than a force play, but if the runner is slow and the third baseman is quick, all the catcher will have to do is apply a tag.

As a coach, though, how can you determine whether or not you have that kind of third baseman? Well, the truth of the matter is that you can't make that determination: at least not at first glance. Watching how a player conducts herself in practice is not the same as seeing how she performs in a game.

You will have to use your judgment here. We have already talked about the kind of makeup needed to play third base. If you have already determined that you have such a player on your team, then chances are she will be able to handle the responsibility of making the right decision when faced with making a play when there are runners on base.

Have confidence in your decision regarding whom you have chosen to play third base, especially when dealing with older players. As the youngsters hit their "tween" years, those who continue to play baseball have more of a sense of what the game entails. Recognizing this sense and exercising good judgment on your part could land you a pretty special third baseman.

First and Second

- If there are runners on first and second with fewer than two outs, the third baseman should look for the bunt depending on who is at the plate.

- A bunt is likely if the top or bottom of the order is up. If the three, four, and five hitters are coming to bat, play back.

- If the third baseman suspects a bunt, he needs to be in on the grass and ready to move quickly.

Runner on Second

- If there are fewer than two outs and a runner on second, the third baseman needs to look the runner back to second after making the play.

- This involves the third baseman fielding the grounder and turning to second base for a split second, letting the runner know that he's aware of his presence.

- The quick look is usually enough to freeze the runner before making the throw to first and recording the out.

THE SLOW ROLLER
The slow ones are often trickier to field than the hot shots

Fielding the slow-rolling baseball is all about reaction time. It takes a quick first step, sure hands, and a keen eye to be able to grab that ball on the move, set and throw to first base all in one seemingly effortless motion.

When coaching youngsters, particularly those under the age of ten, you should not get too down if your third baseman has issues with making this play. There are several factors working against him, mostly physical. For starters, children

that young obviously have smaller hands than older kids, and because of that they have trouble gripping the baseball when picking it up on the fly, which is required for this kind of play.

Also many of them don't have the arm strength to charge a ball and make an off-balance throw. That arm strength usually doesn't arrive until the teen years, and even then accuracy is not guaranteed. That, however, doesn't mean this isn't

The Slow Bouncing Ball

- If the ball is still moving, its destination is unpredictable. Using two hands will allow the third baseman to knock the ball down or keep it in front of him.

- The two-handed method will also allow for a quicker, easier throw to first.

- If a third baseman uses one hand and chooses to swipe at it with his glove, there is a chance he will miss.

The Foul Ball

- If a ball rolls foul and is still near the line, the third baseman should grab it instead of watching it.

- A rolling baseball, particularly one that is on dirt or an edged strip of grass, is unpredictable and can move in any direction.

- If a ball that has rolled foul rolls back into fair territory before it reaches third base (or first base) and no fielder has touched it, it is a fair ball.

a play worth practicing repeatedly.

Simply stand in front of home plate and roll a slow dribbler out toward third. Do this over and over again regardless of the results. If this exercise is done often enough, your third baseman will have a handle on how to make the play mentally. When he catches up physically, it will be fun to watch.

The Off-center Route

- The third baseman should not take a direct route to the ball when it is rolling slowly.

- He should take a slightly curved, off-center approach to the ball, like a mini-arc.

- Players should use the glove hand to scoop the ball and be ready to throw.

- This method will carry the third baseman's momentum toward first base, making the throw easier. A direct route to the ball would make for a more awkward throw.

Eat the Ball

- If there is no play to make, the player should not force one.

- If the third baseman has fielded the ball and has no chance of throwing the runner out, then he should hold onto the ball.

- A forced or rushed throw, particularly if it is obvious that there is no play available, can lead to an error and land the runner on second or third base.

GOING TO THE BACKHAND
Making this play requires a strong arm and special talent

Think of the nursery rhyme about Jack being nimble and quick when discussing the third baseman going to his backhand to make a play. He has to be nimble and quick to make such a play, though jumping over a candlestick is not required. There are some who say it might be easier to do that, however, than to go to the backhand, stay on your feet, and still have the time, balance, and arm strength to make a throw to first base.

This is not an easy play and there is no sugarcoating that fact. A third baseman has to have lightning-quick reflexes to pick up the flight of the ball off the bat and know that he needs to go to the backhand. Picking up the flight of the ball is only half the battle. The third baseman still has to be able to move quickly to his right, bring his glove over, and snag the ball, all while attempting to stay on his feet.

If executed properly, this is one of the prettier plays in

Stay on Your Feet

- Unless the third baseman is playing close to the line, staying on his feet while making the play can often prove difficult.

- By staying on his feet while making the backhanded play, the third baseman has a better chance of throwing out the runner.

- He will not be as rushed when making the throw, which will also be much more accurate than if he had to scramble to his feet or worse yet, throw from his knees.

Pop Up Quickly

- Sometimes diving is unavoidable.

- If the third baseman must be on the ground to field the ball, then he should have a spring in his shoes because he's going to need to bounce back to his feet quickly.

- Most balls that require a backhanded dive are hit hard and therefore afford the third baseman a bit more time to make a throw.

- He should get to his feet as quickly as possible, set, and throw.

baseball and will garner some rave reviews for your third baseman. Not being able to make this play at a young age, however, is something about which a third baseman should not hang his head.

The Big Throw

- There will be situations when the third baseman will not have enough time to get to his feet, set, and make a throw after diving and making a backhanded stop.

- He will have to throw from his knees. This requires a great deal of arm strength and accuracy.

- The third baseman should not attempt the throw from the knees unless he is certain there is a chance at getting the runner. This requires split-second decision-making.

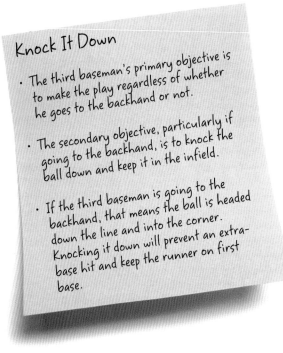

Knock It Down

- The third baseman's primary objective is to make the play regardless of whether he goes to the backhand or not.

- The secondary objective, particularly if going to the backhand, is to knock the ball down and keep it in the infield.

- If the third baseman is going to the backhand, that means the ball is headed down the line and into the corner. Knocking it down will prevent an extra-base hit and keep the runner on first base.

THIRD BASE

FIELDING THE BUNT

The ability to read and react on a bunt is one of a third baseman's greatest assets

A third baseman needs to display quick reflexes on more than just the hot shots and the backhanded plays. He has to be able to anticipate a bunt, charge the ball, and make the play all in a matter of seconds while remembering what to do with the ball once he picks it up.

Natural ability will play a huge role in being able to perform this task, but if you have a cerebral third baseman, one who studies the game, understands situational baseball, and can actually anticipate a bunt, then you have a special player. Nurture him and work with him, because being able to field a bunt capably is something every third baseman is going to need to know how to do as he gets older.

Watch It

- The third baseman needs to watch where the ball is going and quickly determine what route he will take to it.

- If the ball is heading back toward the mound or has not traveled far enough up the line, he should back off in favor of the pitcher or the catcher.

- If the third baseman determines that the bunt is his to field, he needs to take the off-center route to the ball. This will give him enough momentum to make a proper throw.

The Bare Hand

- More often than not, the ball will have stopped before the third baseman reaches it.

- This should be the only time that a third baseman will ever field the ball with one hand.

- Players field this ball with the left foot in front, reaching down with the right arm to grab the ball.

- In the next step, with the left foot still leading the way, the third baseman should step and throw across his body to first base.

If you have a younger third baseman who can get to the ball quickly enough, set, and make an accurate throw to first, you are ahead of the game. The biggest thing to remember, though, is that if you don't have such a player, you must stress to your third baseman that forcing a throw is not an option. If it looks like the runner will be safe, the third baseman should not make a throw simply for the sake of making a throw. A rushed or poor throw could lead to an error or put a runner in scoring position.

One easy way to work with your third baseman on bunting drills is during practice when the rest of the team is practicing bunting. This will give the third baseman ample, stress-free time to work on fielding the bunt, perfecting the little nuances that go along with making the play. It will also give you a chance to observe him in action and make any necessary changes to his approach.

Know the Situation

- The third baseman needs to be aware of what he will do with the ball if there are runners on base and he is fielding a bunt.

- He should listen to his teammates, particularly his catcher. The catcher has the entire field in front of him and has the best view of the unfolding play. He should be yelling at the third baseman as to which base he should throw the ball.

Practice

- It is easy to work on fielding grounders with the bare hand.

- Line up a series of baseballs between the pitcher's mound and the third base line.

- Have the third baseman charge each of them one after another and fire off throws to the first baseman.

- This is a drill the third baseman and a buddy can work on together without the coach or teammates.

THE BASICS

There are certain things a shortstop should have and know before taking the field

Third basemen are the tough ones. Second basemen are the scrappers. Shortstops, well, shortstops are usually the stars, poster boys, you name it, on youth baseball teams. The best athletes usually gravitate toward playing shortstop mostly because they have the arm strength, range, and reflexes required to play the position.

More often than not, shortstops also wind up pitching as well because they possess so much arm strength. Shortstops are usually long and lean, and it's obvious early that they can glide to the ball and make the play.

A coach should not stereotype anyone based on these descriptions. If you have a shorter, stockier player who can

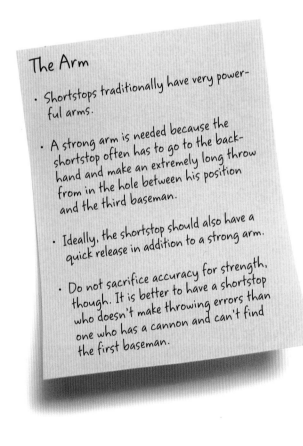

The Arm

- Shortstops traditionally have very powerful arms.

- A strong arm is needed because the shortstop often has to go to the backhand and make an extremely long throw from in the hole between his position and the third baseman.

- Ideally, the shortstop should also have a quick release in addition to a strong arm.

- Do not sacrifice accuracy for strength, though. It is better to have a shortstop who doesn't make throwing errors than one who has a cannon and can't find the first baseman.

The Glove

- The shortstop's glove is small like those of the other infielders but not as small as a second baseman's glove.

- Because the shortstop has to cover more ground than the second baseman, his glove needs to be larger.

- The shortstop will be diving for balls in the hole and up the middle more often than the second baseman, and the extra inch or two on the glove could prevent several base hits over the course of a season.

156

get to the ball and handle the position, by all means put him there. Size and grace do not make a shortstop—talent does. So remember to be open-minded when choosing the shortstop.

Make sure, however, that you have someone who can handle the position. There is a great deal of ground to cover between second and third base and the shortstop is responsible for most of it. He will not be able to get to every ball hit his way, but a good shortstop will have the range to reach a majority of them.

Relating to Second Base

- The relationship between the shortstop and the second baseman is a special one.

- The shortstop needs to be able to communicate with the second baseman constantly, either verbally or through hand signals to determine who will be covering second base on any given play.

- The middle infielders need to work on their respective games together to get in sync. Their relationship must be symbiotic.

Talking with the Catcher

- The shortstop also needs to be a good communicator with the catcher.

- There will be times in the game that the shortstop needs to work out signals with the catcher regarding covering second base on steals and pickoff attempts.

- The shortstop can also signal pitches to the catcher and help call the game to keep the batter off balance.

SHORTSTOP

FIELDING THE GROUNDER

You can have a slick-fielding shortstop if you put in the time and effort

A great fielding shortstop makes everything seem so easy. *Slick* is a word that is often used to describe the ability of the great shortstop. Finding a youngster that falls under the "slick" category can be difficult, though. But there's no need to be discouraged.

Unlike other attributes, such as speed, "slick" is something that can be taught. Start with the two-handed method of fielding a grounder. There is no room for one-handed show-boating when it comes to playing shortstop. Instruct whomever you have playing short to get in front of the ball as best he can, field it with two hands, and make the throw to first—simple, succinct, and to the point.

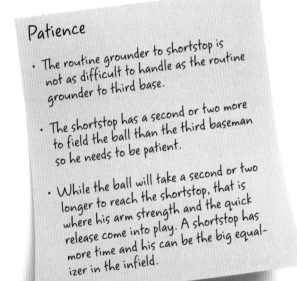

Patience

- The routine grounder to shortstop is not as difficult to handle as the routine grounder to third base.

- The shortstop has a second or two more to field the ball than the third baseman so he needs to be patient.

- While the ball will take a second or two longer to reach the shortstop, that is where his arm strength and the quick release come into play. A shortstop has more time and his can be the big equalizer in the infield.

Be Ready

- The shortstop should prepare for each pitch by dropping down into the ready position, hands on knees, head up, eyes toward the plate.

- When the pitch is thrown, his hands need to come off the knees and down between his legs. He should be on the balls of his feet, rocking slightly and ready to move laterally to either side.

- Often when going into the hole, the shortstop will be on the outfield grass when making a play.

Practice that with him often enough and slick will become part of his lexicon. There is nothing slicker than being able to employ good, solid fundamentals. Flash is fine and is needed once in a while to make certain plays. But fielding the routine grounder doesn't require flash. All it requires is a nice, fluid style.

Before you know it, slick and your shortstop will be synonymous. It is not a difficult concept to grasp. Field the ball. Make the plays. Earn accolades as a solid, error-free shortstop.

Take a Step

- If the ball is hit directly at the shortstop or within a step or two to either side, it is best to take a step in and field the ball rather than wait for it.

- If the shortstop waits for the ball too long, he can get handcuffed, and then it will not matter how much arm strength he possesses or how quick his release is; the runner will still be safe.

Look It In

- As is the case with every other infielder, the shortstop needs to look the ball into his glove and use the two-handed method of fielding the ball.

- Taking one's eye off the ball can result in an error.

- The shortstop should not attempt to make the throw to first until he has complete possession of the ball. This, too, can result in either a fielding or throwing error.

THE THROW FROM SHORT
It takes a big arm and a big effort to get the ball to first from short

Since a shortstop has so much ground to cover, she needs to have an arm that is just a notch better than that of her fellow infielders. This does not make her a better player, more special, or even more talented than those around her. It simply means she has a strong arm, which is generally a prerequisite for playing shortstop.

A shortstop needs to use that arm more because the throws she makes are usually more difficult than the ones made by her fellow infielders. Third basemen have some tough throws to make, especially when they go to the backhand, but on a consistent basis no one in the infield is required to display arm strength as often as the shortstop.

If you have a player who has a cannon for an arm, work with her on refining her skills when making these throws. Often a younger player sacrifices accuracy for power—it occurs frequently with young pitchers, too—and that's a mistake. You

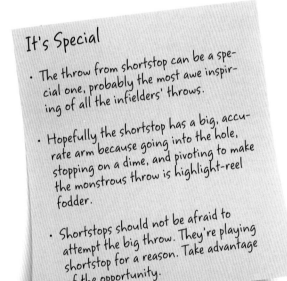

It's Special

- The throw from shortstop can be a special one, probably the most awe inspiring of all the infielders' throws.

- Hopefully the shortstop has a big, accurate arm because going into the hole, stopping on a dime, and pivoting to make the monstrous throw is highlight-reel fodder.

- Shortstops should not be afraid to attempt the big throw. They're playing shortstop for a reason. Take advantage of the opportunity.

Overhand

- Teach shortstops to throw the ball overhand.

- If the shortstop throws the ball sidearm or three-quarters, it is simply laziness.

- A throw that isn't made overhand isn't as strong

and will often lead to the runner beating out the grounder.

- When making a sidearm or three-quarters throw, the shortstop is also more likely to pull the first baseman off the bag, resulting in an error and a runner reaching safely.

can have power and be accurate. It just takes a little work.

It is true that many of the plays a shortstop makes are of the bang-bang variety, thus limiting her time to make a throw. As her coach, you need to remind her constantly to stay calm and just make the throw. Do not worry about the runner; do not worry about making an error. Too much thinking is no good for any player, especially one whose performance will so often fall under a microscope.

Also, be sure that your players are warmed up when they take the field. If the shortstop's arm isn't loose, it could be problematic. That would be the case for any position, but it becomes particularly glaring if your shortstop is bouncing throws 10 feet in front of first or throwing them 10 feet above the first baseman's head.

The View

- The shortstop has the best view of the runner heading toward first or second base. The whole play unfolds directly in front of him.

- Because the shortstop can see the entire play unfolding, he knows how much time he has to make a play.

Therefore there is no reason to rush a throw to either base.

- The shortstop should know his arm strength and his limitations. Being able to see where the runner is will aid him in coming to these realizations.

Don't Panic

- Making a throw across the infield is not a reason to panic.

- Panicking leads to throwing errors. Shortstops should stay calm and focused on the first baseman. It's just the two of them playing catch.

- If the shortstop keeps that thought in his head, the anxiety that some feel when readying to make a throw will be lessened.

THE BALL IS IN THE AIR
Who's got it? Does anyone have it?

Catching a simple popup is one thing. A shortstop, however, is in the unique position of having to cover a sizeable piece of real estate, worry about what his teammates are doing, and still be able to concentrate on catching the ball. Sometimes it is not easy being able to put all those things together.

This, however, is a perfect opportunity for you to challenge your shortstop. Put him to the test and have him take charge of the situation. Explain to him that many popups are his responsibility, whether they are behind third base or in the infield. At the very least, he should have a hand in who does catch the ball.

He needs to be the chief overseer, the traffic cop, whatever moniker you wish to give him. But he needs to be vocal and take charge of the situation, knowing when to make the play and when to allow himself to be called off.

Confusion when fielding a popup occurs often when

Behind Third Base

- The shortstop should call off the third baseman when there is a popup behind third base.

- The third baseman has to backpedal or turn to run and get under the ball. The shortstop has a much better angle to the ball.

- Picture a triangle when thinking of the shortstop's route to the ball. The shortstop's route to the ball may be the longest side of the triangle but it presents the easiest route to getting under the ball.

Listen to the Outfielder

- While the shortstop has a better angle than the third baseman on a popup behind third, he doesn't always have a better angle than the left fielder.

- If the ball is hit deep enough into the outfield, the shortstop needs to be cognizant of the left fielder and listen to determine whether he is being called off the play.

- The outfielder coming into a ball has an even better angle than the shortstop, who is making a diagonal movement.

dealing with youngsters. Mostly that is because no one is willing to take charge or understands what it means to take control of the situation. As a result, the ball falls in between a group of players who wind up pointing fingers and saying, "I thought you had it." Don't let that happen. Give your shortstop the power to take control.

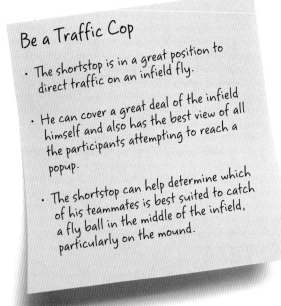

Be a Traffic Cop

- The shortstop is in a great position to direct traffic on an infield fly.

- He can cover a great deal of the infield himself and also has the best view of all the participants attempting to reach a popup.

- The shortstop can help determine which of his teammates is best suited to catch a fly ball in the middle of the infield, particularly on the mound.

Vocalize

- The shortstop should not be afraid to call someone off when chasing down a popup.

- He is in a take-charge position and has the best opportunity to cover the most ground on an infield pop. Therefore he needs to use his voice and call off the pitcher, third baseman, and second baseman when he sees fit.

- The shortstop should shout and have everyone clear out in order for him to make the play.

SHORTSTOP

163

THE HOLE
There are no shovels required to cover this hole

Let's clarify. The hole about which we speak is not a physical hole per se. No one has taken a shovel and dug a little ditch into which your players will dive. Rather, the hole is an area on the field. It refers to no-man's land deep between second and third base to the right of the shortstop and between first and second base to the left of the second baseman.

While making either play is difficult, a second baseman making a play in the hole has a much easier time of it than a shortstop does. He has more time and a shorter throw to first base. When a shortstop goes into the hole, the play takes on a much different feel because the degree of difficulty is much greater.

For a shortstop to consistently make this play, he has to have a good feel for the position and an innate ability to move quickly without thinking. Reflexes are important, because once the ball is hit, the shortstop needs to be on the move

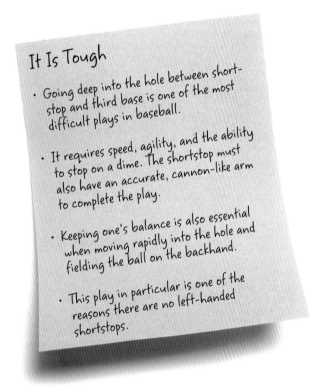

It Is Tough

- Going deep into the hole between shortstop and third base is one of the most difficult plays in baseball.

- It requires speed, agility, and the ability to stop on a dime. The shortstop must also have an accurate, cannon-like arm to complete the play.

- Keeping one's balance is also essential when moving rapidly into the hole and fielding the ball on the backhand.

- This play in particular is one of the reasons there are no left-handed shortstops.

The Path

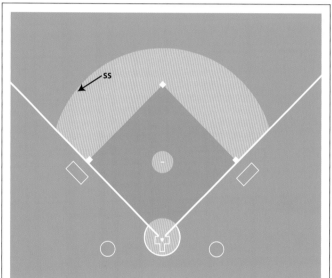

- Taking the correct path to the ball is essential in making this play.

- Often the ball is hit so hard that cutting across the diamond in a straight line toward third base is inadvisable because the ball will be behind the player before he reaches it.

- Instead the shortstop should travel at an angle—think triangle again—away from the batter. This will give him a few extra seconds and likely mean he's fielding the ball on the outfield grass.

immediately, for there is little time to waste.

Practicing making this play is not terribly difficult. The coach, or any player, can simply hit ground balls into the hole and the shortstop can attempt to field them. What a coach cannot teach is speed and arm strength. Either a shortstop has the range to get to the ball or he does not. Either he has the arm strength to stop and make the throw from deep in the hole or he does not.

When we speak of a special player taking up shortstop, this is part of what we mean. It takes a gifted athlete to be able to glide into that no-man's land, grab the ball, and make the perfect throw to first. It won't happen every time he fields a ball hit there, but more often than not a good shortstop won't give a coach any reason to worry when he ranges to his right.

The Plant

- When the shortstop is traveling at full speed, planting the foot to make a throw is difficult.

- Usually, the shortstop will slide as he fields the ball, either on the grass or the edge of the dirt. Players should go with the slide and plant the foot, if the right foot is the lead foot.

- It is easier to slide into the backhanded play while leading with the right foot.

The Jump Pivot

- If the shortstop is leading with his left foot when he has fielded the ball, then he should come down on that foot and make a jump/pivot/throw.

- The shortstop needs to jump off his left foot and pivot in the air, making the throw as accurately as possible.

- This is a bang-bang play with no time for thinking about it. It is one of the more spectacular plays a shortstop can make but requires quick instincts and decision-making ability.

THE DOUBLE PLAY

The double play is a often called a pitcher's best friend, and with good reason

Whenever players can get two for the price of one, they should take advantage of the situation. However, just because the double play is there for the turning doesn't mean it will actually be executed. This is the type of play that takes timing, skill, and a great deal of practice.

If you want a good double play combination in the middle of your infield, then you are going to have to work just as hard as they are to make it happen. That means grounders, lots of them. This is the type of play that can only get better through repetition and familiarity between the players involved.

Your middle infielders will have their own unique styles. To be able to turn a double play together, though, they have to

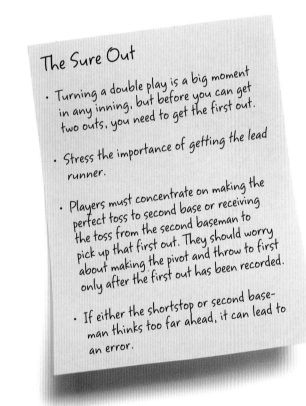

The Sure Out

• Turning a double play is a big moment in any inning, but before you can get two outs, you need to get the first out.

• Stress the importance of getting the lead runner.

• Players must concentrate on making the perfect toss to second base or receiving the toss from the second baseman to pick up that first out. They should worry about making the pivot and throw to first only after the first out has been recorded.

• If either the shortstop or second baseman thinks too far ahead, it can lead to an error.

Accepting the Throw

• The shortstop needs to be able to accept the throw from the second baseman in stride.

• If the throw is made perfectly—and it should be chest high—the shortstop should easily be able to glide across the base, catch the ball as he touches the base for the force play, and complete the throw to first for the double play.

• When making the throw to second base, shortstops should throw the ball to the base and not make the receiver of the ball work to get the throw.

be able to act as one unit. That means thinking alike, knowing what the other person will be doing, how they will react when the ball is hit or thrown their way, and how they will handle getting the ball to you.

So work with them. Hit them grounder after grounder, directly at them, in the hole, up the middle, everywhere they could possibly make a play. A double play isn't called a pitcher's best friend without reason. But for the pitcher to benefit from the twin killing, it has to be turned, and that won't happen without some hard work.

Underhanded

- If the throw is shorter—usually less than 12 feet—players should not be afraid to toss it underhanded.

- There is no need to rifle a ball at whomever is covering the base.

- Players should keep the wrist firm and scoop the ball to the fielder waiting at second base, making sure the elbow is tucked in close to the body when making the toss.

Throwing across the Body

- Often when turning a double play, a shortstop will have to charge a ball and then make a throw after he has fielded the ball on an angle that puts him parallel to or in front of second base.

- At these times he will have to make the throw across her body. This is one of the few times that it will be acceptable to make a sidearm throw to the base because physically it would be difficult to stop and make an overhand throw.

SHORTSTOP

167

INFIELD FLY RULE
What is it and what should players do when an umpire calls for it?

There are two sides of the situation here and both employ a simple principle—do not get cutesy. Infielders need to catch the ball regardless of the situation while baserunners need to stay put and not take any needless chances.

Here is why. The umpire will invoke the infield fly rule when there are fewer than two outs and runners on first and second or when the bases are loaded. When this play is called, the batter is automatically out. This rule was instituted to ensure good sportsmanship. Otherwise, an infielder could settle under a popup, feign catching it, and let it drop in an attempt to turn a double play or force the lead runner out.

By enforcing this rule, the umpire eliminates the chance of that happening. But infielders must be aware of the rule, and that has to come from the coach. As players get older, it should be easier for them to understand what this rule involves, both literally and conceptually.

Being Aware

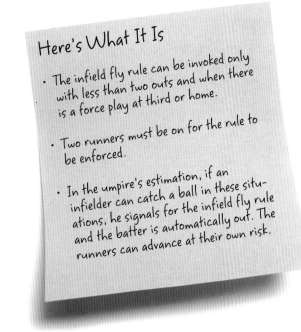

Here's What It Is

- The infield fly rule can be invoked only with less than two outs and when there is a force play at third or home.

- Two runners must be on for the rule to be enforced.

- In the umpire's estimation, if an infielder can catch a ball in these situations, he signals for the infield fly rule and the batter is automatically out. The runners can advance at their own risk.

- The infielders as well as the runners need to be aware of the situation.

- Players must know how many runners are on base and how many outs there are.

- Infielders should meet before the game so they have a plan of attack should the umpire invoke the infield fly rule. Each infielder has to cover his respective base should a runner try to advance.

Explain the rule and its ramifications in great detail to your players, because they need to understand it not only from an infielder's perspective but from that of the runner as well. Runners have been caught trying to advance on an infield fly because they believe they are being stealthy and will catch the infield napping. That usually isn't the case. Most older players are so familiar with the rule that it is virtually impossible to advance unless the infielder drops the ball or it bounds away from him.

So stress to your players not to take chances. It won't pay off on the bases and it won't make a difference on the field. Catch the ball, stay on the base, and wait for the next batter to step into the box.

The Umpire

- Players should look and listen for the umpire. He will signal an infield fly with his arm but he will also call out that the infield fly rule is being invoked. Players should pay attention to what the umpire is doing and where he is stationed.

- It is at the umpire's discretion that the infield fly rule will be invoked. Players should not assume that he will signal for it just because there has been a popup to the infield.

Don't Get Cute

- Infielders should make an honest effort to catch every ball within the vicinity of their positions. It's better to be safe than sorry.

- Players should not get cute and let the ball drop simply because the infield fly rule has been invoked.

- If a player attempts to bait the runners by letting the ball drop, they can advance at their own risk and anything can happen, including having the ball skitter away.

SHORTSTOP TIPS
A tiny, helpful hint can go a long way toward making a better player

While we detailed the ins and outs of playing shortstop in the previous chapter, we left out a few things because they were applicable only to older players and how they approached the game. While some of the concepts discussed in this segment could probably be of benefit to younger players, our belief is that they have enough to handle trying to learn how to play the position and the game. Getting fancy is something that's best left for players over the age of ten who have

been playing for a while and have a better rate of retention.

When working with shortstops at an older age, you need to explain to them in greater detail that they have more responsibility than their younger counterparts. A solid shortstop can be a game-changer, one who understands that turning a double play properly and not just shoving the ball over to second base in hopes of retiring the runner can be of great benefit to the team.

Beginning the Double Play

- A shortstop cannot turn the double play without getting the first out, and he cannot get the first out without fielding the grounder to short.

- Teach your shortstop to concentrate on making the initial play; get the sure out

and worry about eliminating the lead runner.

- If he makes a good throw to second base, the second baseman will complete the double play, but that can't happen unless he focuses on making the initial play.

The Left Foot

- The shortstop has fielded the grounder and is now ready to make the move to second.

- The shortstop should keep the right foot planted firmly but pivot on it so that the left foot now moves back, opening the body to the second baseman.

- The front of the body should be facing the base with the left foot planted closer to the outfield grass.

- Players should stay on the balls of their feet and not get caught flat-footed.

There are certain aspects of footwork when turning a double play that older players can employ to make the play easier. While dragging the left foot back and making the body square to second base might be a bit awkward at first, it will consistently result in a better throw than if the shortstop simply whipped her arm across her body.

This little tip will result in a well-rounded infielder, one that can not only handle her position but make the second baseman a better player as well. If the second baseman realizes that every throw she gets from the shortstop will be well devised, accurate, and easy to handle, she will be a much better player for it.

The Transfer

- Ideally, the shortstop has fielded the ball with two hands, using the bare hand to cover the ball in the glove.

- He needs to make sure the ball is in the glove before trying to grab it and make the transfer; otherwise an error could occur.

- The shortstop should grab the ball with the bare hand and prepare to throw to first, taking his time and making sure he has a proper grip on the ball.

The Throw to Second

- The shortstop must make sure to actually throw the ball to the second baseman and avoid getting cute and trying to flip it with the glove.

- The throw to second should be strong enough that the second baseman can make his own transfer with it and attempt to complete the double play. The shortstop should not short-arm the ball or throw it too softly.

- A shortstop can use his judgment and toss it underhanded, if close enough.

PLAYING THE INFIELD IN
A gamble that can pay huge dividends or be a complete bust

The older players get, the more they have to understand strategy and how it impacts the outcome of a game. When a coach or a manager commits to playing the infield in, it can have great ramifications. This defensive alignment can prevent an important run from scoring or, if the ball is hit hard enough, backfire and wind up costing the team on the field several runs.

Playing the infield in occurs when a coach or manager brings his four infielders onto the edge of the grass in front of their respective positions in hopes of knocking down or fielding a ground ball, thus preventing a runner from scoring from third base. If the field you are playing on doesn't have grass, move your players to where the cutout should be.

More often than not, a manager or coach will use this strategy to prevent the tying, go-ahead, or winning run from scoring late in the game. It is a bit tougher to bring the infield

Be a Student

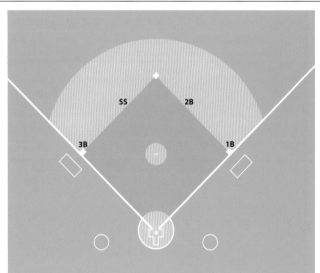

- Understanding the game and when the situation calls for the infield to be played in is important.

- Discuss strategy with your players and let them know why playing the infield in can be effective. Explain the pitfalls as well.

- Ultimately, the coach will decide when to move the infield in, but the players can have input if they understand the decision-making process and what is at stake.

Going Home

- The purpose of playing the infield in is to prevent a run from scoring, so the ability to make the throw home is essential.

- Accuracy is an important part of making the throw to the plate. The throw cannot pull the catcher off the base, leaving him unable to make the force play or a tag.

- This can be a nerve-wracking play for the infielder. He should be patient and set himself properly before making the throw.

in when playing in an aluminum bat or composite bat league because the speed at which the ball travels off the bat can make it dangerous. It's a bit safer in a wooden bat league.

That, however, is the coach's call. If you have a good enough fielding infield, the speed at which the ball comes off the bat might not matter. It is your job as coach to determine when you think your team, specifically your infield, is ready to handle playing the infield in. Just because it is a sound strategy to employ, that doesn't always mean it is worth using. Some teams do not have players capable of handling the ball at such a close range.

Either way, it's worth discussing with your team and employing from time to time to see how they can handle the pressure.

Look the Runner Back

- If the infielder has fielded the ball cleanly, there is a chance the runner will not take off from third.

- Once the infielder has the ball, he needs to take a second to check the runner back to third if he hasn't run. This will take a split second and still allow the infielder time to make a proper throw to first base if there is no force play at the plate.

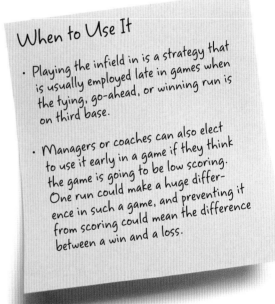

When to Use It

- Playing the infield in is a strategy that is usually employed late in games when the tying, go-ahead, or winning run is on third base.

- Managers or coaches can also elect to use it early in a game if they think the game is going to be low scoring. One run could make a huge difference in such a game, and preventing it from scoring could mean the difference between a win and a loss.

173

HOLDING RUNNERS ON SECOND BASE

Keep your friends close but the opposition closer, particularly when they are on base

Learning how to keep a runner close when he is on second base is a bit trickier than when a runner is on first base. For starters, neither the shortstop nor the second baseman can stand on the bag, arm outstretched waiting for a throw from the pitcher, as the first baseman does. It's not practical. Even if the pitcher were to throw over as often as he does when a runner is on first base, the infielder in question could never get back to field his position properly should the pitcher opt to make a pitch.

An attempt to pick a runner off second is almost always a timing play. The best way to get better at it is to practice it—repetition, repetition, repetition. The infielders need to

Signals

- The middle infielders have to communicate to determine who will be covering second base in the event of an attempted pickoff play.

- They can signal each other or communicate verbally. Either way, they should let the pitcher know who will be there to receive the throw.

- The middle infielders should also have a signal system set up with the catcher to alert him when they feel a pickoff attempt is required.

Getting There

- When attempting a pickoff, it isn't always easy for the shortstop to make his way to the base.

- The shortstop needs to be as stealthy as possible and stay out of the runner's line of sight.

- To do this, he should take a bit of a circular route behind the runner, on the outfield grass, and sneak into the base as quickly and quietly as possibly. More often than not, the runner will be paying attention to the pitcher and the hitter and not have a good view of the shortstop.

become familiar with each of your pitchers and their body language. They need to become familiar with the signals they will employ to decide who will cover the base or for when the catcher will be making the long throw on an attempted pickoff at second.

The pitchers also need to feel comfortable when throwing the ball to second base on a pickoff. Because it is a timing play, the pitcher will often spin and throw before the infielder gets to second base. He has to trust that his teammate will be there to receive the throw and that the ball won't simply end up in center field and the runner on third base.

The movements made by right-handed pitchers and those of left-handed pitchers on a pickoff throw to second are different. Give your players time to work on receiving throws from both if you have a lefty on your staff. You don't want the first time a player sees a pickoff move to be in a game situation when a runner is in scoring position.

The Fake

- Bluffing a runner is a very effective way to keep him close to the base.

- The shortstop and the second baseman need to work their way in behind the runner and get close enough to pound their hands in their gloves. Usually this will be enough to coax a runner into moving back to the base.

- If the runner hears the infielder and believes him to be nearby, chances are he won't stray far off the base.

The Tag

- When the infielder takes the throw from the pitcher, he needs to position himself between the runner and the base.

- The infielder should accept the throw from the pitcher and immediately put as much of his body down between the base and the runner as possible, preferably dropping to one knee so the runner cannot reach the base with his hand or foot.

- Providing less of a target for the runner will make it easier to record an out.

EXTRA WORK

A little hard work never hurt anyone, particularly when it comes to playing the infield

There is no substitute for a good attitude and a strong work ethic, whether we are talking about a coach or a player. Some players are blessed with natural ability while others have to work harder to hone their skills. If the players with lesser skills have a good work ethic and are willing to put in the extra time, then there is no reason why they should not be able to compete with the more gifted players.

It is all about hard work. If the player is dedicated and willing to put in the time and effort, then you, as a coach, have to be there for him, willing to put in the time and effort as well. Building a better ballplayer is not a one-way street. Sure, a player can go to the batting cage and work on a few things

On Your Knees

- Have the third baseman kneel on the infield grass at third base.

- Throw sharp ground balls to him, bouncing them just before him. Make them difficult to field so he takes some of them off his arm and chest.

- This isn't an easy drill for the infielder—he can get bruised as well—but it will improve his reflexes and his quickness when fielding a ground ball.

Extra Infield

- There are few things as enjoyable as taking infield practice, so do more of it.

- If you have an infielder that's having trouble fielding grounders, get him to practice early or keep him late and hit grounder after grounder to him.

- The repetition and extra work will do wonders for the troubled fielder. It can also be of huge benefit to the fielder who already has a handle on how to play the position.

to improve his performance at the plate, but you have to be part of the equation as well.

If you have gone into coaching, you obviously love what you are doing and enjoy working with the kids. The work should not stop, though, just because practice has ended. No ballplayer is perfect. Everyone can use the extra work, so ask for volunteers.

Check with the kids and their parents and see who wants to stay a little longer and get some extra infield practice in. Most kids will enjoy the one-on-one attention and thrive in a setting where they are getting more personal instruction, even if that simply means hitting your second baseman grounders for an extra fifteen minutes every day.

The hard work will be well worth it, and the reward for putting in the effort will be evident not just by what you see on the field but in what you learn about your players as you teach them of the benefits brought on by taking an extra step.

Taking the Relay

- Infielders need to know how to take a relay throw from the outfield.

- The infielder on the base to which the ball will be thrown should line the cutoff man up with the outfielder fielding the ball.

- The infielder who ultimately receives the throw should be yelling, telling the cutoff man whether to move to line up with the outfielder.

- The cutoff man should be positioned perpendicular to the outfielder so he can receive the throw before stepping into his own throw back to the infield.

A Relay to Home

- On many plays, the first baseman will move across the infield to receive the throw from the outfielder.

- The other infielders, however, need to be able to work the cutoff and line up based on the catcher's instructions.

- The infielder needs to listen for the catcher's instructions on where to go and whether they should cut the ball off or let it through to the plate.

HELPFUL HINTS

There are always little things that can be done to make a ballplayer better

If you have players that are not as gifted as others—and what coach doesn't have a few—then there are some helpful little tips that can be offered to make them seem just a bit more skilled than they actually are. These tips will appear to be strokes of genius on your part but in actuality they are just common sense baseball practices that time and experience would have eventually provided.

These helpful hints will be of benefit only if the player in question chooses to employ them. Point out through example, though, how something as simple as taking a step one way or another can make a big difference when making a play. Those extra 2 or 3 feet an infielder moves in either

Lateral Movement

- You cannot teach speed but agility can be improved through some hard but simple work.

- Have the infielder you are working with go to his position and move laterally from side to side, back and forth, extending the distance he must move each

time. It will resemble doing wind sprints.

- Now have him field the ball while doing this. Throw one to his left and make him get it, and as he's fielding it throw one to his right. Go as fast as he can tolerate it, but make sure he fields the ball.

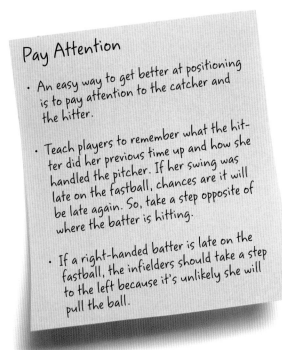

Pay Attention

- An easy way to get better at positioning is to pay attention to the catcher and the hitter.

- Teach players to remember what the hitter did her previous time up and how she handled the pitcher. If her swing was late on the fastball, chances are it will be late again. So, take a step opposite of where the batter is hitting.

- If a right-handed batter is late on the fastball, the infielders should take a step to the left because it's unlikely she will pull the ball.

direction can mean the difference between the winning run scoring and the winning run never making it past third base.

Stress to your team the importance of having a high baseball IQ. Practicing the game is one thing. But learning about it, experiencing it, watching and understanding it are entirely different matters all together. The players who see their baseball IQ improve are the ones who think, analyze, and pay attention. They don't walk off the field after practice and head home, not thinking about the game until the next time they are on the practice field.

The biggest helpful hint you can provide your players is to encourage them to become well-rounded players. So much will fall into place if they simply immerse themselves in the game and study it. The physical things we will discuss in this portion of the chapter will help, but they cannot replace common sense or an analytical mind that will play out scenario after scenario until a perfect solution to the problem at hand is achieved.

Take a Step Back

- Players should not be afraid to take a step onto the outfield grass for certain hitters.

- Some big hitters can smoke a baseball, particularly down the first or third base lines. For these hitters, have the infielders take a step back onto the outfield grass.

- The extra step or two backward will buy the infielder a precious second or two that could make all the difference in whether or not he fields a hard-hit ground ball.

Throw from the Knees

- Have your infielders on their knees in various spots throughout the infield.

- Have them work on throwing to each of the bases when on their knees.

- There will be several points in a game during which an infielder will be required to make a throw from his knees, whether it's a shortstop going to third base after making a diving stop or a first baseman going to second after making a similar play.

THE POSITIONS
Finding the right player for the right position takes some time and effort

Finding someone to patrol your outfield can be as difficult a task as finding players to fill your infield. Each of the three outfield positions requires a different set of skills and a different mindset, so it is important for the coach to determine quickly which of his players will be capable of handling these responsibilities.

When your players are a bit younger (under ten years old), locking them into one position in the outfield isn't advisable because they still have much to learn. If you feel you have a future outfielder, then expose him to all three outfield positions in an effort to find out which one suits him best. By getting a feel for what all three positions are like, your players

Center Field

- The center fielder is in charge in the outfield.

- He is generally the quickest of the three outfielders and the best defensively because he has more ground to cover. He doesn't necessarily have the strongest arm of the three.

- The center fielder should call off the other outfielders on close fly balls.

- Because he has so much responsibility and it is such a coveted position, center field should be played by someone who displays leadership qualities.

Right Field

- While the center fielder doesn't need to have a strong arm, the outfielder with the cannon is usually placed in right field.

- The right fielder has the longest throws to third base and home plate, and if he

has a strong enough, accurate arm, he will be able to keep runners from advancing a base or scoring.

- Right field is a very strategic position, one that requires an alert, well-schooled player.

will have a better understanding of what their teammates are encountering during the course of a game.

These different perspectives will help them as they get older and eventually claim one outfield position for themselves. As the players get older, they generally display an affinity for one position. If you have a leader who can cover ground, for example, stick him in center field. The big arm goes in right and the well-rounded youngster can patrol left field. The older they get, the easier it will be to determine positions.

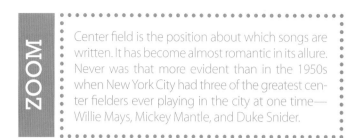

ZOOM

Center field is the position about which songs are written. It has become almost romantic in its allure. Never was that more evident than in the 1950s when New York City had three of the greatest center fielders ever playing in the city at one time— Willie Mays, Mickey Mantle, and Duke Snider.

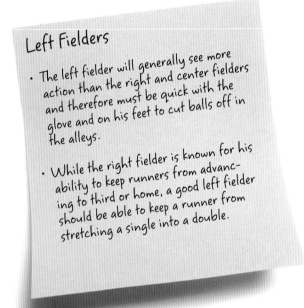

Left Fielders

- The left fielder will generally see more action than the right and center fielders and therefore must be quick with the glove and on his feet to cut balls off in the alleys.

- While the right fielder is known for his ability to keep runners from advancing to third or home, a good left fielder should be able to keep a runner from stretching a single into a double.

No Man's Land

- The left and right fielders need to be cognizant of the Bermuda Triangle that exists between him, the first or third baseman, and the foul lines.

- This area is generally where popups fall in for base hits because there is confusion as to who should catch the ball.

- Ideally, the shortstop or second baseman should take a diagonal path to the play and make the catch, but if they can't, the corner outfielder needs to be aggressive and make the play.

GETTING READY
Preparing to play the outfield is just as important as preparing to play the infield

When they are younger, infielders will almost always get more of the attention. That's because so few balls are hit on a fly to the outfielders or over the outfielders' heads. But the outfielders still need to be aware of what to do and how to do it should the ball come their way.

By the time youngsters reach middle school, the fly balls will be coming and the outfielders will be more than just window dressing on a field. They will need to know how to catch a fly ball, what to do with it when men are on base, etc. So do not ignore the outfielders when they are younger.

The stereotypical, Hollywood notion is that you stick the worst player in right field where he can do the least damage.

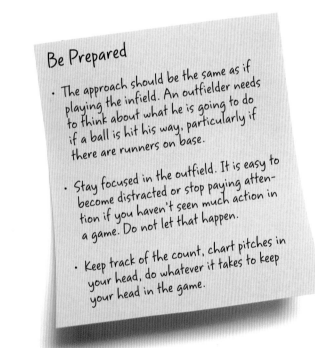

Be Prepared

- The approach should be the same as if playing the infield. An outfielder needs to think about what he is going to do if a ball is hit his way, particularly if there are runners on base.

- Stay focused in the outfield. It is easy to become distracted or stop paying attention if you haven't seen much action in a game. Do not let that happen.

- Keep track of the count, chart pitches in your head, do whatever it takes to keep your head in the game.

Get into Position

- The ready position in the outfield is similar to that of an infielder, just not as intense.

- The outfielder should have his hands on his knees as an infielder does and be ready to break after the ball quickly in any direction.

- The outfielder shouldn't be standing upright with his hands at his side. This will make getting a jump on a ball hit his way more difficult. It's easier to spring into action from the ready position.

But if you treat a youngster that way in real life, you will lose him emotionally. Work with your outfielders as much and as intensely as you do your infielders, because even though they won't see as much action early on in their careers, they will someday.

As a coach, you want them to be prepared for the next coach who will teach them. Don't let that coach or your players down by neglecting your outfielders at a young age.

YELLOW LIGHT

Sometimes it is difficult for an outfielder, particularly at a younger level, to keep his head in the game. Few balls get hit his way, especially if the pitcher is dominant. It becomes easy for him to let his mind wander. Remind your outfielders to stay focused as often as possible.

Finding the Ball

- Locating the ball off the bat can sometimes be difficult, especially if a player has no experience doing it.

- Outfielders should focus on the batter and watch him swing. When he begins his stride, the player should be ready for a ball to be hit his way.

- The outfielder needs to take into account sun, wind, backdrop and all other conditions before each inning in an effort to pick up the ball off the bat better.

Ready to Run

- When the pitch is thrown, the outfielder needs to be ready to move and fast.

- Based on where the ball is hit, the outfielder should be moving to where he thinks it will be coming down.

- If a ball is hit on the ground to an infielder on his side of the field, the outfielder needs to move in quickly and back up that infielder should the ball get through into the outfield.

COMING IN ON A FLY

Keeping the ball in front of you is the most important aspect of charging a fly

Judging where a fly ball is headed is probably one of the toughest things for a young outfielder to do. Far too often you will see a youngster barrel in after a ball only to have it go over her head. It can be embarrassing for the player and cost your team a few runs.

Never get down on your outfielder if this happens and do not let her teammates ride her, either. Mistakes happen and sooner or later everyone will make an error. Proper preparation will cut down on the frequency with which those errors occur. A good way to start off is by having your outfielders, particularly the younger ones, play deep. The chances of a ball getting hit over their heads will be slim, and it is always

Watch It

- Teach kids not to take their eyes off the ball once it has left the bat.

- They need to watch its flight and make the determination on where they have to go to catch the ball.

- Outfielders must pay attention and avoid being

fooled. Often an outfielder will break the wrong way on a ball because he did not get a good read on it off the bat. The outfielder will have a second or two to determine which way the ball is going.

Call a Player Off

- When coming in on a popup, the outfielder always has the right of way ahead of the infielder.

- It is easier to charge in on a ball and make the play than it is for the infielder to backpedal.

- Outfielders should scream loudly "I got it" or "Mine" so the infielder knows to back off the play.

- Collisions can occur and serious injuries can result if an outfielder doesn't call off the infielder loudly.

easier to come in on a ball and play it on a hop rather than deal with worrying about running into the fence.

Also, spend time hitting fly balls to your outfielders. Let them get a sense of what the ball looks like coming off the bat and the sounds it makes when it travels certain distances. Good outfielders, particularly when they get older and begin using wooden bats, should be able to use sound to judge how far or how well a ball has been struck.

YELLOW LIGHT

Willie Mays made the basket catch popular in the 1950s and for a decade, kids were imitating him and coming home with a bruised chest. Do not let your players try the basket catch. Not only can they get hurt, it is also easier to drop the ball when not attempting to catch it properly.

Get It Up

- An outfielder should not let his glove hang down at his waist when charging in for a fly ball. The flight of the ball is unpredictable and outfielders need to be prepared.

- The outfielder should have his glove up and out in front of him when coming in on a ball. This way if the ball is not caught on the fly, it can be caught on one hop. Otherwise, there is a chance the ball can skip by.

Two Hands

- Outfielders should always use two hands when catching a pop fly, regardless of whether they are charging in or standing still.

- Discourage hotdogging the popup or attempting to catch it with one hand, off to the side, or in a basket catch.

- Proper form involves settling under the ball, having the glove hand and throwing hand up, and squeezing the ball tight once it is in the mitt.

185

GOING BACK

Do not get caught flat-footed or heading in the wrong direction when chasing down a fly ball

Teaching a young ballplayer how to go back on a ball can be tricky. For starters, children under the age of ten, unless they are baseball junkies, have a tough time with their sense of direction when going back on a fly ball. The child who sits and watches games with Dad and always has a ball and glove in his hand will have an easier time understanding what it means to successfully go back to get a fly ball.

Those who do not have as much exposure will have problems, and it will be obvious watching them twist and turn as they attempt to determine where the ball is going, where it will land, and what is the best way to get there.

You can start by having them get in the ready position and

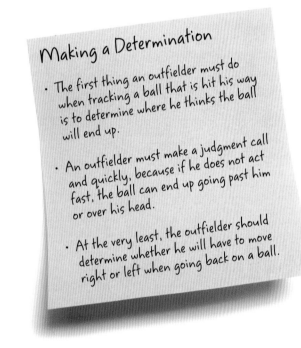

Making a Determination

- The first thing an outfielder must do when tracking a ball that is hit his way is to determine where he thinks the ball will end up.

- An outfielder must make a judgment call and quickly, because if he does not act fast, the ball can end up going past him or over his head.

- At the very least, the outfielder should determine whether he will have to move right or left when going back on a ball.

Breaking After the Ball

- If the outfielder is in the ready position when the ball is pitched, it will be easier for him to jump into action when the ball is hit.

- The outfielder should begin running to the spot where he thinks the ball will come down.

- Experience will be the best teacher in determining ball speed, distance, and how quickly the outfielder needs to run to get under the ball in time to make the catch.

then simply turn sideways and run while looking over their shoulder. Repeat this drill several times and then have them turn the other way and perform the same drill. After they've repeated it several times, you will have a better sense of which outfielders are more coordinated and which ones will require extra work.

Now you can practice by hitting shallow fly balls to them. Don't start with towering popups; these can be intimidating. Go slowly and work your way up, stressing that catching the ball isn't what the drill is about initially. Finding the proper route to the ball is more important because if you don't get to the ball, it won't matter whether or not you can catch it.

Hit fly balls to either side of the outfielder so they have to practice going back to the right and to the left. If they are right-handed, some might find it difficult to go back the other way and vice versa. That's okay. This drill is designed to make them feel more comfortable and become accustomed to going back on a fly ball in every direction.

Watch the Ball

- Teach players to *never* take their eyes off the ball while it is in flight.

- There are very few outfielders who have played the game that are capable of putting their heads down, running to where they think the ball will wind up, and then looking up to make the catch.

- Players should practice running while looking up. The first few times outfielders may feel uncomfortable not looking where they are running, especially if the field is poorly maintained.

Settling Underneath It

- The outfielders that are smooth always seem to glide under the ball before making a catch.

- Gliding under the ball does not mean being casual. The outfielder needs to set up under the ball once he has determined where it will come down and be prepared to make the catch with two hands.

- A one-handed catch is acceptable if the outfielder is still moving or has to reach to catch the ball.

187

THE SUN
Keeping the sun out of your eyes is imperative when playing the outfield

Even the best of outfielders can have problems with the sun. You cannot catch what you cannot see, and if that bright ball is blinding you, then there is not much that can be done other than get out of the way and wait for the ball to find earth.

When dealing with younger players (under the age of ten), the chances of a ball being hit high enough for the sun to come into play are remote. Most children that age lack the power to launch shots high into the air. It is when the players become a bit older and learn how to handle a bat better that the sun becomes an issue. When it does, the simplest method to help your players deal with the sun is to provide them with sunglasses.

Sunglasses

- Older players should be allowed to wear sunglasses if it makes them feel more comfortable catching a fly ball.

- Avoid having the younger players wear sunglasses. It can cause an unneces-sary distraction at an age when the kids have enough trouble staying focused.

- Very few younger players will hit a fly ball high enough or far enough to warrant the outfielder wearing sunglasses.

The Glove and Hand

- The best defense for dealing with the sun is to use the glove or the hand as a shield.

- If using the glove, players should raise it so that it is cutting across the face lengthwise and folded shut. They can peek over the edge of the glove, glancing over as much as possible without being blinded by the sun.

- If using the hand, players should hold it up to shield their eyes. They can look over the hand as with the glove or between the fingers. They should find a method that is most comfortable for them.

Sunglasses are not to be played with when standing in the outfield, and they aren't to be used in an effort to gain style points. They are an aid to help the outfielder—or the infielder— keep better track of the balls that are hit in the air. Employ the use of sunglasses judiciously, though.

If the sun is behind the outfielders or it's a late evening game, the glare might not be strong enough to require sunglasses. We say this only because the youngsters on the field don't need any other distractions, which the sunglasses will provide.

The best method, though not the simplest, of dealing with the sun is to teach them how to shield their eyes. Also pay close attention if your team plays night games. Many of the children will not be used to playing under the lights, and the glare could cause problems like the ones caused by the sun.

Don't Look

- It's common sense, but make sure your players know that looking directly into the sun can be dangerous.

- They should watch the flight of the ball out of the corner of their eye but never track the ball directly in the sunlight.

- Suggest occasionally glancing up in between pitches to check for cloud cover or to determine if the sun's position has changed.

Cover Up

- There is no reason to get hurt when fielding a fly ball.

- Instruct the outfielders that if they lose a ball in the sun, there is no shame in covering up.

- Have them put their glove over their heads and cover themselves so that if the ball does hit them, they won't be severely injured.

- Have them scream "I lost it" when they have lost sight of the ball in the sun.

MAKING THE THROW
Learning how and where to throw the ball will make an outfielder complete

Teaching a player where to throw the ball is just as important as teaching him how to throw it is. Any player with a strong arm can whirl and fire a ball back to the infield without much regard for where it will wind up. It takes a smart, fundamentally sound ballplayer to know where the ball needs to be.

Encourage your outfielders to throw ahead of the runner, thus preventing him from taking an extra base. Make them hit the cutoff man, because a wild throw can be just as damaging if not more so than no throw at all. A strong arm means nothing if they do not know how to harness that energy and strength. If every throw winds up against the backstop behind the catcher, what good is having a strong arm?

Proper Alignment

- When the outfielder has settled under the ball and is about to catch it, he needs to have his body aligned properly to make the throw.

- This means he should be standing perpendicular to the infield with his glove foot forward and his throwing foot back. Outfielders should never catch the ball with the glove behind them; they should always have it in front with the throwing hand up and ready to pull it out.

Taking the First Step

- Chasing down a fly ball will not always provide enough time to set up properly. But when the outfielder does have time, the best method for throwing is to take a step into the ball as he catches it.

- If the outfielder is aligned properly and has his glove up, the step will give him the needed momentum to make the throw once he pulls the ball out of his glove.

Most times the throw to the infield involves a bang-bang play, leaving the outfielder with precious little time to think, let alone act. That's why it is imperative that they take a few seconds before each pitch and think about what they will do if the ball is hit their way. A little bit of preparation and some common sense will go a long way to making your players better outfielders.

Using Two Hands

- This is something that is often forgotten by younger players. Two hands are a must.

- It will be easier to make a throw if the bare hand is already up by the glove instead of down by the out-fielder's side. The second or two it takes the outfielder to bring his free hand up is precious time wasted.

- Using two hands will also make it easier to catch the ball and lead to fewer drops.

Hitting the Cutoff Man

- Hitting the cutoff man is of the utmost importance because it can prevent a runner from advancing an extra base.

- An outfielder must use his head when making a throw back to the infield. If a runner is clearly going to score, he should not try and air a throw out to reach home. Instead, hit the cutoff man to prevent the player who just got a hit from advancing a base.

- Unless the outfielder is already close to the infield, he should always hit the cutoff man with a throw.

CARING FOR YOUR ARM
Take care of your arm and it will take care of you

The responsibility of caring for a pitcher's arm should fall mostly on the player. But when that player is a child, she doesn't always know the difference between right and wrong. That is where the coach comes in.

As the responsible adult in the equation, the coach needs to make sure that her pitchers take proper care of their arms. This means watching pitch counts, limiting the frequency with which they pitch, and also warming them up and cooling them down properly. Some youngsters are naturally rubber-armed and seem as if they can throw for days without any repercussions. The more you throw, though, the more damage is done to the arm.

Pitching is not a natural motion for the arm, and the stress it causes can do serious damage, regardless of a player's age. Far too many "tweens" and teenagers have undergone elbow surgery because they have damaged ligaments after

Warm Up Properly

- Teach pitchers not to pick up a baseball and expect to start firing fastballs at top speed with the first pitch.

- A pitcher's arm should be warmed up slowly, starting with a few soft tosses, then moving to long tossing.

- Only after the long tossing should they start throwing the ball harder. After a few hard tosses, they can begin pitching out of a windup and throwing with their regular motion and speed.

Pain

- There will always be some general soreness associated with pitching, but experiencing pain is not part of the equation.

- If a pitcher feels pain when throwing, regardless of where the pain is or how severe, he needs to stop immediately and tell the coach or a parent.

- The pitcher should not try to be tough and pitch through the pain. This can lead to a more severe injury.

throwing too much or attempting to get too fancy with their pitches too soon.

Remember that these are children and their bodies are still growing. Do not overuse or abuse them. Let them develop and fill out naturally, and over time they will hopefully become the types of pitchers you think they can be.

Icing

- There is a debate as to whether icing after throwing is actually a good practice.

- Some icing is not a bad idea, particularly in the elbow and shoulder because it promotes blood flow to the area, which leads to a quicker recovery time.

- Too much ice, however, can impede the recovery time according to some experts.

- After pitching, some simple exercises involving arm movement will do as much if not more to help the healing process as icing.

Rest

- So you've thrown a hundred pitches and your arm is tired. Rest it.

- A pitcher, unless properly conditioned to do so, should not be throwing on back-to-back days.

- Starting pitchers need several days of rest in between starts for a reason—they need to give their arms time to heal.

- Some throwing in between starts is advisable, but throwing at full force for a prolonged period of time is not recommended if the player has just pitched at great length in a game.

193

GETTING STARTED
It takes some time to prepare for a stint on the mound

Pitchers are a different breed. They enjoy the spotlight, relish the chance to be the center of attention, and are usually ready to handle the heat when something goes wrong—because they are used to getting blamed when it does.

More so than their teammates, pitchers must be creatures of habit, though. They need to be repetitive in everything they do, from the way they stand on the mound to the way they wind up and even in how they follow through or fall off the mound after making a pitch. This act of repetition will benefit the pitcher in that, if he is instructed properly, he will be more consistent in everything he does on the mound.

The slightest variation in setup, delivery, or follow-through can alter the pitch, changing not only where it ends up but how it gets there. So drill the notion of consistency into your pitchers. Help them find what is comfortable and effective for them and make them repeat the process over and over again.

Setting Up

- Right-handed pitchers begin setting up by placing their right foot either on or against the rubber, and vice versa for lefties. One foot has to be touching the rubber at all times, and that foot is used to push off when pitching.

- The pitcher cannot be on the mound and touching the rubber if he is not in possession of the ball. This rule is in place to prevent the pitcher from deceiving a baserunner who might take a lead thinking the pitcher has the ball.

Finding the Target

- Once the pitcher has stationed himself on the rubber, he should locate the catcher's target and focus in on it.

- Try to block out any distractions. This is the time in the pitching process when the pitcher begins to hone in on the plate and the batter, running over his game plan in his mind.

- The pitcher should pay attention to which side of the plate the catcher is setting up on.

Remember that proper preparation is essential for every aspect of the game but it is particularly important when it comes to pitchers. An infielder or an outfielder may be able to get away with varying his routine from time to time. Pitchers, however, need to be the most consistent players on the field for each and every pitch.

GREEN ● LIGHT

When preparing to pitch, it will benefit a pitcher if he does a little tidying up each time he takes the mound. His opponent will not have the same length of stride as he does. Therefore the landing area on the mound will have to be doctored after every inning. Teach your pitchers to do a little housekeeping to make sure the mound is always in shape.

The Signs

- This will usually only apply to older pitchers, though some youngsters are proficient enough on the mound and are capable of throwing several different pitches at several different speeds.

- The catcher will put down a finger or several fingers between his legs with the number of fingers corresponding to a predetermined pitch. For example one finger is a fastball, two fingers is a changeup, etc.

- The pitcher will either agree with the catcher or shake off the sign until he gets a pitch he likes.

Beginning the Windup

- There are several ways to wind up with a pitch: The windmill style that you see old films of players from the 1940s and 1950s using with regularity, and pitching from a set position during which the hands never break contact are the two most popular.

- The pitcher may choose either of these methods but should not be married to them. Ultimately, he has to find what is comfortable and works best for him, then stick with it.

THE WINDUP

Whether rocking or pumping, windmilling or staying conventional, the windup is crucial

Some pitchers will spin and gyrate on the mound as they go into their windup, doing all kinds of crazy things in an effort to distract the hitter. If they are comfortable and effective pitching this way, there is no reason to change it.

But when you are teaching a youngster how to pitch, the best course of action is to keep it simple and traditional. Do not get fancy and do not get too complex. Pitching itself is complex enough. The more time you spend sticking to the basics, the better off your young pitchers will be. As they get older, become more experienced on the mound, and get a better sense of how to pitch and what works for them, then they can experiment with their deliveries, whether that

The Beginning

- Once the pitcher has received his signals from the catcher, he can begin the windup, which he will use if there are no runners on base.

- The pitcher begins by facing the batter, holding the hands together at the waist.

- Once the pitcher is on the rubber, he must keep his hands together. If he wants to separate his hands, he must first step off the rubber or he will be called for a balk.

Going Up

- Depending on the windup the pitcher employs, he will now bring his hands over his head.

- If he is using the windmill style, he will begin to swing his arms backward then bring them forward and join them over his head.

- If the pitcher is using the more conventional windup, his hands will remain in contact.

- He will take a slight step back with his left foot, then begin to move forward, never breaking contact between the rubber and his right foot.

means becoming a sidearm pitcher or someone who completely spins around on the mound.

For now, though, the best bet is to keep it simple. The object for these youngsters is to simply get the ball over the plate. They have plenty of time to worry about style later on.

The following windup is for right-handed pitchers. Left-handed pitchers will go through the same delivery except they will be facing first base, have their left foot touching the rubber, etc.

PITCHING

Pivoting

- As the pitcher begins to bring his hands down from over his head, he will begin to bring his left leg and knee up into his chest.

- While bringing the left leg up and in, he will also pivot on the right foot—never breaking contact with the rubber—so that his body is facing third base as he goes through his delivery.

- The hands should be together and drop no lower than the bottom of the rib cage before separating in preparation to deliver the pitch.

Fluidity

- The windup should be fluid and rhythmic, not herky-jerky and jagged.

- The pitcher should look graceful on the mound, almost as if he is performing in a ballet.

- The best way to make sure the windup and delivery remain fluid is through repetition. Pitchers can practice going through the windup even if they are not actually throwing.

STRIDING

Taking that big step is the first step toward becoming a better pitcher

The stride a pitcher takes is unlike any other in the game. It is not like the steps a runner takes when circling the bases, nor is it similar to that of a position player as she moves to field a ball.

It is simply not spontaneous. The stride a pitcher makes is contrived and controlled, repeated over and over again as many as one hundred times a game. It is explosive and important and needs to be consistent in order for the pitcher to be effective. While a runner can stride at less than 100 percent and still accomplish his task, a pitcher has no such luxury. Her stride, though fluid and graceful, must be made with maximum effort on each and every pitch if the delivery is to be effective.

Pushing Off

- The movement of beginning the windup creates momentum and generates the needed power to push off the rubber.

- As the body rotates, the pitcher should be leaning back slightly so that she slingshots forward when pushing off the rubber.

- The back foot should now be parallel to the rubber, pushing up against it after the pitcher has pivoted.

The Stride

- After the pitcher has brought his left leg into his chest and begins pushing off with his right leg, he can begin striding forward with his left leg.

- The lead (left) foot should be angled down slightly.

- At this point, the hands are still together in the glove and the ball remains out of the batter's sight.

- The front leg should ultimately swing from third base toward the hitter and come down on the mound well in front of the rubber.

This is why it is so important for a pitcher to have strong legs. Her power comes from her legs regardless of whatever lightning she may have in her arm. So strengthen your pitchers' legs. Have them run, have them jog, have them trot in between games, before practice and after practice. Have them build up the strength in their legs because it is what will carry them on the mound.

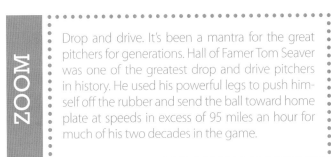
PITCHING

Beginning the Pitch

- As the pitcher is striding toward the plate, his arm should be cocked and begin to come forward just as the front foot touches down.

- The left leg should be bent, almost at a right angle, and the two feet should be at their farthest distance apart.

- The left foot and leg will pull the body forward while the right foot continues to push off the rubber.

Full Extension

- When the right leg is fully extended, the pitcher is in a position to release the ball.

- Depending upon the pitcher's arm slot, his hand should be between 12 and 15 inches out in front of him when he releases the ball.

- The front foot needs to be planted firmly as it pulls the body forward. The pitcher will begin to shift his weight forward at this point in the delivery.

RELEASE & FOLLOW-THROUGH

Where the pitcher releases the ball will determine where it will end up

A pitcher's release point, his follow-through, and his landing need to be consistent on each pitch. There are several reasons for this—the most important of which is that he can't become a good pitcher if he does something different on every pitch. There is no justification or acceptable reason to have a pitcher change his delivery and motion over and over again.

If one of your pitchers finds a delivery and motion that is successful, have him stick with it and make sure that he does not change his routine. Work with him in practice to perfect his delivery. You do not want to send him out to the mound if he is not confident that he can perform the same motion pitch after pitch.

The Back Leg

- As the pitcher releases the ball, his right foot should break contact with the rubber and begin to swing around to the front of his body.

- Depending on the action of his delivery, his foot/leg could be only an inch or two off the ground or it could be as much as 2 feet.

- A pitcher's size and comfort level will have some impact on his follow-through. Regardless, he needs to keep his balance as he swings his right foot around.

The Pitching Arm

- Once the ball has been released, the arm must follow through completely.

- The pitcher should not stop the arm motion, jerk his arm back in a violent motion, or attempt to short-arm a pitch.

- Teach pitchers to follow through and let the arm fall naturally through the delivery so that when the pitch is completed, the arm is crossing and or pointing at the opposite foot.

If a pitcher changes his delivery because he is hurt or feels discomfort, sit him down immediately. Changing one's delivery to favor an injured foot, leg, hip, etc. will simply cause an injury to another part of the body. So keep an eye on your pitchers and make sure they tell you when they are not feeling well or if something is bothering them.

Finally, a proper follow-through is also important because it will determine how a pitcher lands and whether he will be in a position to make a play once he has made the pitch. The pitcher needs to bear in mind that he is also a fielder and is responsible for anything hit back his way or in front of the mound. Therefore, if he is falling off the mound in a crazy or uncontrolled fashion, it will make it more difficult for him to field a ground ball or get his glove up on a line drive.

Maintenance

- We have talked about mound maintenance and this is why: If you bring the front foot down into a soft spot or place on the mound that has not been manicured, then an injury can occur. The pitcher can twist an ankle or wrench a knee.

- The pitcher should take a few seconds before each inning and check his landing area, smoothing it out and filling in any divots created by the opposing pitcher.

Overstriding

- A pitcher should not attempt to take a 10-foot stride on 5-foot legs.

- An overstride can cause the pitcher to lose balance, which will result in a poor pitch.

- If a pitcher overstrides, he could strain a muscle or tear a ligament. Make sure the pitcher stays within himself and does not get too over-zealous when delivering a pitch.

THE PITCHES

Having a vast array of pitches will help the player as he develops from a thrower to a pitcher

Teaching a youngster how to pitch is one of the most difficult tasks a coach can perform, simply because many coaches do not know how to pitch themselves. The best advice that we can give to prospective coaches when it comes to teaching pitching is to find an assistant coach who pitched during his career. It will be much easier for him to discuss the finer points of pitching with your older players.

The younger players do not require as much instruction and therefore do not really need a pitching coach. Many of them do not have big enough hands to grip the ball properly, so trying to teach them how to throw a knuckleball, screwball, split-fingered fastball, etc. is pointless. When dealing with

Two-seam Fastball

- Grip the ball with the index and middle finger together between the two rounded seams at the top of the baseball.

- The thumb should be underneath the ball with the fourth and fifth fingers supporting the outside of the ball.

- This fastball has a tendency to sink and is not as powerful as the four-seam fastball.

- When throwing this fastball, it must be kept lower in the strike zone to be more effective.

Four-seam Fastball

- This is the money pitch for power pitchers.

- Grip the ball with index and middle finger together across the top of the seam.

- The thumb is placed underneath the ball but the ball is not jammed back into the crux between the thumb and the index.

- There should be a gap between the ball and that crux. Squeeze the ball with your fingertips; do not smother it.

younger kids, show them the two basic fastball grips and find one of the myriad changeup grips with which they are comfortable.

Most pitchers under the age of ten cannot grasp the concepts involved with pitching because at this point they are still throwers rather than pitchers. Many of them simply have trouble throwing the ball over the plate. Work with them on finding the plate and learning the strike zone, and when they get older they can work on mastering different pitches.

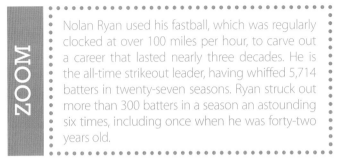
The Changeup

- The changeup is a nice complement to the fastball.

- There are several grips that can be employed when throwing the changeup, but the pitch's real effectiveness lies in the arm speed of the pitcher.

- The arm speed with a changeup looks like a fastball is being thrown, but because the elbow moves ahead of the wrist during the delivery, the ball is heaved toward the plate more than it is thrown.

The Slider

- The slider can be a great weapon for a pitcher but should not be used by power pitchers.

- Throwing a slider with great frequency will take away from a power pitcher's speed.

- The slider looks like a fastball coming out of a pitcher's hand but actually has late break on it and can tail away or into a hitter quickly and unexpectedly.

- Sliders can cause arm strain and should not be taught to younger players.

THE CURVEBALL

The great debate about the curveball has been raging for years

Let the debate begin. There are some who believe the curveball is verboten, a blight on youth baseball that needs to be abolished. They point to injuries resulting from throwing the pitch as the evidence in their case to abolish it.

That is archaic thinking, according to some recent studies. The general consensus among youth coaches, administrators, and even doctors these days is that the curveball is not the problem that causes so many issues with young pitchers.

Injuries and arm fatigue come from overuse rather than throwing the occasional curveball.

It is an interesting debate, one that can be argued well on either side. Based on all the available evidence and research, placing the blame for elbow and other arm injuries solely on the curveball seems a bit like horse-and-buggy thinking. Most local Little Leagues haven't banned the pitch. Rather, they have instituted pitch counts to keep unscrupulous

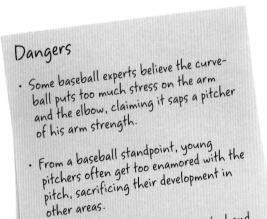

Dangers

- Some baseball experts believe the curveball puts too much stress on the arm and the elbow, claiming it saps a pitcher of his arm strength.

- From a baseball standpoint, young pitchers often get too enamored with the pitch, sacrificing their development in other areas.

- The pitch is very difficult to control and master and shouldn't be used in a game until a pitcher is able to handle it.

The Grip

- The ball is wedged deeper into the hand than with the fastball, pushed back into the space between the thumb and forefinger.

- The index and middle fingers are placed together with the middle finger directly over the seam of the baseball.

- The thumb is also along a seam on the bottom of the ball.

- The pitcher should be holding the ball tighter than if he were using a fastball grip.

coaches from overusing a dominant pitcher.

That would seem to have more of an impact in terms of limiting injuries than telling a thirteen- or fourteen-year-old that he cannot throw a curveball. Is the arm action involved with throwing a curveball a bit more stressful than a changeup? Sure. But so is that of a fastball, so why such a fuss?

The bottom line is that you, as the coach, need to decide what you want your pitchers to do. If you say no curveballs, then it is no curveballs. If a parent does not have a problem with his son breaking off a few curveballs, then he can work on them at home with Dad or when he is away from the field.

It is an interesting debate, though, one that will get some people riled up pretty quickly. Educate yourself, though, before making any decision about how you want your pitchers to approach using this very tricky pitch.

The Motion

- Learning the arm motion is difficult when throwing a curveball.

- Right-handed pitchers move the arm forward in a right-to-left motion, jerking their arm downward as they follow through.

- The wrist should snap downward and the ball should roll out of the hand, over the index and forefinger with the middle finger applying most of the pressure on the ball. The index finger is used more as a guide.

Mastering the Pitch

- Learning the ins and outs of throwing a curveball properly can take *years*, not days, weeks, or months.

- A young pitcher should work on building up his arm strength before attempting to master the curveball.

- Coaches should not allow their young pitchers to ignore developing their other pitches in order to focus solely on the curve. It will limit them as pitchers.

WORKING THE HITTER
Knowing how to work a hitter can make a pitcher nearly impossible to hit

The best part of pitching is the challenge it presents. Anyone can get on the mound and throw the ball as hard as she can while hoping for the best. It takes much more to be a pitcher and not just a thrower.

A pitcher employs a strategy. She studies hitters and understands what pitches she can use to get them out. It's a chess match for the pitcher and not just a matter of throwing the ball by the hitter. As a coach, this can be an exciting and fun time for you as well because you get to teach a young pitcher all about strategy, working the corners, working the count, or about throwing a waste pitch when it is an 0-2 count just to try and get the batter to bite.

Working with the Catcher

- The pitcher cannot work the hitter alone. He needs the catcher's input and help to properly attack a hitter.

- The catcher and the pitcher need to study the opposition as well as possible and work together to develop a game plan as to how they will pitch to each batter.

- As pitchers get older, they will learn to keep "a book" on opposing hitters, writing down what has worked and what hasn't against them.

Pitching Inside

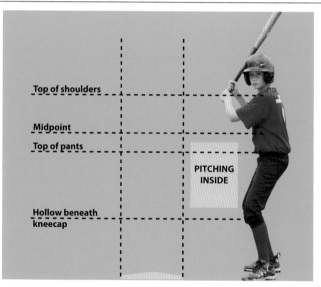

Top of shoulders

Midpoint

Top of pants

Hollow beneath kneecap

PITCHING INSIDE

- A pitcher has no weapon as effective as being able to come inside on a hitter.

- If a pitcher can control his fastball, he can pitch inside and keep a batter off the plate.

- Most young hitters have trouble catching up with a good fastball. When it is thrown inside, it is virtually unhittable.

- A pitcher can be very intimidating if he pitches inside, giving the impression he will hit the batter if he gets too close to the plate.

Above all other aspects of the coach's job, this is where he can really have the chance to shine and dive headlong into the game with his players. Teaching a pitcher how to work a count can lead to hour-long discussions of strategy and change the way a young pitcher approaches the game. Enjoy this part of the game because there are few aspects that are as rewarding as teaching a youngster how to pitch.

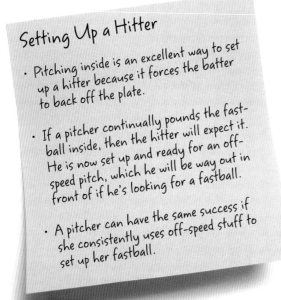

Setting Up a Hitter

- Pitching inside is an excellent way to set up a hitter because it forces the batter to back off the plate.

- If a pitcher continually pounds the fastball inside, then the hitter will expect it. He is now set up and ready for an off-speed pitch, which he will be way out in front of if he's looking for a fastball.

- A pitcher can have the same success if she consistently uses off-speed stuff to set up her fastball.

Working the Corners

- Working the corners is another way to set up a hitter.

- By pitching a batter inside consistently, he will come to expect the inside pitch.

- It is then that the pitcher needs to throw a pitch, regardless of what that pitch is, on the outside corner.

- The pitcher need not be perfect with his location to make this an effective strategy. He simply has to be able to move the ball around the plate.

THE SIGNS

Learning to give and read signals can make a battery a very effective duo

Catchers and pitchers need to be able to work together. It is essential for the success of the team. They need to be able to communicate verbally and nonverbally on a level that the other players on the team aren't required to do. The pitcher and the catcher are involved in every play of the game and share a much more intimate relationship, and therefore must be able to get along well also. Like any couple that is close, there will be disagreements from time to time. The catcher will call for a pitch that the pitcher doesn't necessarily want to throw and occasionally fireworks will ensue.

It is your job as coach to find a catcher that communicates well with the pitchers and to make sure the pitchers

Work with the Catcher

- Older pitchers who have the opportunity to call their own game will have to work out signals with the catcher.

- The catcher holds one finger for a fastball, two for a changeup, etc.

- There are no set assignments to correspond

pitches and fingers. It should be whatever works for the pitcher and catcher and makes them comfortable.

- The pitcher and catcher should also work out signs for pitchouts, pickoff throws, etc.

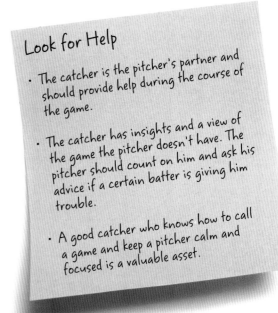

Look for Help

- The catcher is the pitcher's partner and should provide help during the course of the game.

- The catcher has insights and a view of the game the pitcher doesn't have. The pitcher should count on him and ask his advice if a certain batter is giving him trouble.

- A good catcher who knows how to call a game and keep a pitcher calm and focused is a valuable asset.

understand that the catcher is there to do a job.

This is a two-person show. Sure, the pitcher can be throwing a whale of a game. But if the catcher isn't there to guide him through it, then that whale of a game might not happen. Learning the signs and figuring out how to communicate is an essential part of the relationship between the pitcher and his battery mate, one that is often underrated or overlooked.

ADVANCED PITCHING

Watch the Target

- The pitcher needs to trust his catcher's instincts. He needs to pay attention to where the catcher has set the target and called for the ball.

- If the pitcher does not trust the catcher or does not throw the ball to where the target is set up, he can cross the catcher up. If the catcher calls for an inside changeup and the pitcher throws an outside fastball, the ball will likely end up at the backstop.

Just Say No

- While the pitcher needs to turn to the catcher for help, he does not have to do everything the catcher asks of him.

- The pitcher has the ability to shake off the catcher if he calls for a certain pitch. In fact, the pitcher needs to be comfortable making the pitch, so being able to stand up to the catcher and call him off is important.

- A pitcher should explain to the catcher in between hitters or innings why he just shook him off.

209

PITCHING FROM THE STRETCH

Cutting down on time to the plate will help keep runners from stealing a base

Often young pitchers will be pitching out of the stretch not because there are men on base and not because they understand the concept involved with cutting down the time it takes to get to the plate. They simply pitch from the stretch because it is what is comfortable for them and what works, and this is all right.

Having younger pitchers, particularly those under the age of eight, pitch from the stretch is a better idea anyway. The less movement these younger players are required to make, the easier it will be for them to find home plate. The gyrations involved with going into a windup, keeping one's balance, and firing the ball toward the plate are often too much for

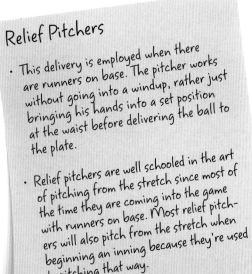

Relief Pitchers

- This delivery is employed when there are runners on base. The pitcher works without going into a windup, rather just bringing his hands into a set position at the waist before delivering the ball to the plate.

- Relief pitchers are well schooled in the art of pitching from the stretch since most of the time they are coming into the game with runners on base. Most relief pitchers will also pitch from the stretch when beginning an inning because they're used to pitching that way.

Time, Precious Time

- Pitching from the set position also saves precious time when there are runners on base.

- The last thing a pitcher wants to do when there is a runner on base is waste an extra second or two, giving that runner more of an opportunity to steal a base.

- By pitching from the stretch, he can get the ball to home plate quicker, giving his catcher the extra time needed to throw out a would-be base stealer.

210

the little ones to handle. So let them throw from the stretch as often as they like. Also, most leagues at that age do not allow runners to lead or steal bases, so the reason for pitching from the stretch is lost anyway.

As the pitchers get older, however, and begin dealing with baserunners who can lead and steal, the concept of pitching from the stretch needs to be explained in great detail. For the older pitcher, it is not a difficult idea to grasp—cut down on your time to home plate so the runner cannot steal a base.

But if you are not a pitching coach, or do not have one on your staff, try to find one who can effectively teach your older pitchers the slide step. It is a quicker way to the plate that takes a great deal of practice and the proper instruction to perfect. But if the twelve- to fourteen-year-olds you have on your team get a sense of how to use it and what it does—particularly if you are fortunate enough to have an accomplished pitcher—then the slide step can be a very effective weapon in their arsenal.

No Windup

- Remember that it is not advisable to go into a windup when the situation calls for pitching from the stretch.

- There are situations that allow for the windup when there are runners on base, though. If there is a runner on third or if the bases are loaded, chances are the runners will not be moving, particularly early in the count. It is at these times that it is safe to abandon pitching from the stretch.

The Slide Step

- Like so many other aspects of pitching, the slide step is difficult to master.

- It involves not lifting the front leg as high in the kick and moving it a bit quicker to home plate, in effect sliding toward the plate.

- While not an actual slide of the foot, the motion does allow for the pitcher to move more quickly to the plate and does afford his catcher an extra second or two to throw out would-be base stealers.

PICKOFFS
An important weapon for advanced pitchers

When a pitcher allows a baserunner either via a single or a walk, he generally will have no one to blame but himself. He can, however, make amends and correct his own mistake with a strong pickoff move.

There is so much going on in a game with young pitchers—learning how to find the strike zone, worrying about giving up base hits, and worrying about walking hitters—that developing a good pickoff move seems like the last thing they should be working on. After all, it is something they will not need until their middle school and teen years when opposing players are taking leads and stealing bases.

Having younger players explore the pickoff move will not hurt their development, though. It will actually enhance it by making them well-rounded players while giving them a proper foundation for when they move on to playing in older leagues. Being cognizant of every aspect of the game will

Righties I

- Right-handed pitchers have a more difficult time with the pickoff to first than left-handed pitchers because they do not have the clear view of the runner that the lefty does.

- The right-handed pitcher must turn his head and look over his left shoulder to get a glimpse of where the runner is. He must telegraph his interest in the runner, while the left-handed pitcher never has to move his head, only his eyes.

Righties II

- The right-handed pitcher must step toward first base when attempting a pickoff throw or he will be called for a balk.

- The step should be an extremely quick, short step with the pitcher pivoting on his back foot.

- The throw must be a quick snap of a throw because of the time it takes to make the pivot.

- It takes time for a right-handed pitcher to master the footwork and timing to perfect a pickoff throw to first.

make them complete ballplayers.

You may find that you have your hands full with your team as it is and that none of your pitchers are ready to take on the challenge of working on a pickoff move. That is fine. Keep an eye out, though, for that special youngster that has the poise and presence on the mound. He'll be the one that will benefit the most from adding this special move to his repertoire.

Lefties

- Left-handed pitchers have a naturally easier time making a pickoff throw to first base.

- They are already facing the base while on the mound and have a better view of the runner than right-handed pitchers.

- It is easier to fake the delivery home and step toward first base to make the pickoff throw for a left-handed pitcher.

- Most of the great pickoff artists are left-handed.

No Balk

- It is physically impossible to balk when going to second base on a pickoff throw.

- The average fan is not aware of this and will usually scream "balk" when a pitcher makes a throw or fakes a throw to second base on a pickoff. The average fan is wrong.

- The pivot foot has to disengage the rubber in order to throw to second, and once the pivot foot has moved, there is no balk.

FIELDING
Great fielding pitchers grab it, knock it down, or slow it down

While some pitchers spend many hours worrying about what to do when they are throwing the ball, many of them have no idea what to do when the ball is hit their way. It can be difficult for young pitchers to put the complete package together when on the mound, particularly if they are playing in an aluminum bat league.

The ball comes off the bat so quickly that there is very little reaction time for older teens and adults. So many youngsters are simply lost when it comes to fielding the ball on the mound. Treat pitchers like any other infielder. Work with them and have them go through infield drills like their teammates. Not only will this help hone their fielding skills when they play other positions, it will also give them valuable practice time in picking the ball up off the bat.

Some parents insist that their young pitchers wear heart guards when they are pitching because of the balls that are

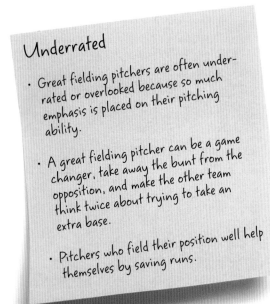

Underrated

- Great fielding pitchers are often under-rated or overlooked because so much emphasis is placed on their pitching ability.

- A great fielding pitcher can be a game changer, take away the bunt from the opposition, and make the other team think twice about trying to take an extra base.

- Pitchers who field their position well help themselves by saving runs.

Approach

- The pitcher should put aside for a moment that he is a pitcher and approach the game as an infielder.

- When fielding the ball, all the rules that go into making a good infielder apply to the pitcher—be prepared, look the ball into the glove, etc.

- A pitcher needs to be careful, though, particularly in an aluminum bat league. Balls travel back through the box at great speeds and if the pitcher doesn't have great reflexes, he could get hurt.

hit back through the box. Don't ever argue with a parent on this topic because ultimately it is the parent's decision to make regarding the welfare of the child. Provide your opinion and give the reasons why you are pro or con, but never question the parent's judgment when it comes to someone else's child.

Back It Up

- The pitcher needs to be aware of what is happening when there are runners on base so he can back up the play.

- If a runner is moving from first to third on a ball hit to the outfield, the pitcher needs to back up third base in case the throw gets through.

- Likewise if there is a runner on second base and there is a play at the plate.

PFP

- Pitcher's fielding practice is usually only seen in spring training around Major League teams but is something that needs to be done often by players at every level.

- The pitcher simulates throwing a pitch as the coach hits grounders into the hole at first base. The first baseman fields them and then leads the pitcher, who is running to cover, to the base with the throw.

- This exercise is something that should be done with pitchers every week.

RUNNING TO FIRST BASE

A batter should never let up when running to first base

Hustle. When put together, those six letters spell the word that is of paramount importance when playing baseball. Players need to know that they have to hustle at all times. Never is that credo more important than when on the base-paths, particularly when running to first base.

One of the more basic principles that a coach must impart to his players from the first day of practice is that they need to hustle down to first base on every ball that is hit. Run full out every time. There is no excuse for taking a play off or not running out a batted ball. A runner never knows what will happen when the ball is hit. If she assumes the shortstop or third baseman will make the play, then she could be left jogging down to first when the infielder in question bobbles the ball, but has time to recover and make the play because she hasn't run.

Do not tolerate a lackadaisical attitude toward running the

Run Full Speed

- Players should not assume that a popup or a ground ball will be an out when it is hit.

- Errors occur, so every batter should run out every ball hit at full speed regardless of the point in the game or the score.

- By running quickly a batter can force a fielder into making a bad throw.

- It is unacceptable to trot down to first base or not give 100 percent at all times.

Run Past First

- When running to first base, the runner should not slow down as he approaches first base.

- The runner should be aggressive and continue to run at full speed.

- The runner never knows if a throw will go wide or if the first baseman will drop the throw, so he needs to run past the base at full speed rather than pull up and risk being called or tagged out.

bases. In fact, it's a good idea to instruct runners to run to first base even if they have walked. Not only does it present a good image, it will ingrain in them a spirit and approach to the game that will last a lifetime.

Do Not Turn

- If there is no intent to turn and head toward second base, the runner should run straight through the base and up the first base line.

- The runner should not make a turn toward second base unless intending to go to second base. A runner can be tagged out if he

turns toward second and the first baseman thinks he is attempting to advance a base.

- The runner should either run up the foul line or veer off into foul territory after passing the base.

Making the Turn

- If the batter has recorded a base hit and will clearly have a chance at going to second base, he needs to approach first differently than he would if he were trying to beat out a base hit.

- The runner needs to run in foul territory toward first

and begin his turn as he approaches first base.

- Just before first base, the runner should take a step or two to his right and run through first in a way that puts him on a direct path to second rather than running straight through the base.

BASERUNNING

217

STEALING SECOND BASE

A little thievery can go a long way toward making your charges better ballplayers

Stealing bases can be a real game-changer in youth baseball, regardless of whether we're talking about nine-year-olds or fourteen-year-olds. Younger players often panic when faced with the prospect of throwing out a would-be base stealer, resulting in throws that either wind up in the outfield or get dropped.

While it may seem a bit unfair to paint all young infielders with this brush, the fact remains most Little Leaguers who attempt to steal a base end up being successful because the pitcher, the catcher, and the infielders—or some combination thereof—have not done their job properly. If you have a fast player on your team, exploit his speed. He has it so let him use it.

Watch the Pitcher

- A player should watch an opposing pitcher carefully in order to pick up quirks in his delivery and to determine whether or not he telegraphs a pickoff move to first base.

- When the runner is on first or second base, he needs to study the pitcher further and determine quickly when it is the right time to steal a base.

- Unless directed to do so by the coach, the runner should not steal on his own.

Stay Alert

- The runner needs to stay focused and pay attention, because if he lets his mind wander he will be an easy target for a pickoff attempt.

- When on base, the runner also needs to be alert in the event of a wild pitch or a passed ball in order to determine whether the ball has squirted far enough away from the catcher to allow him to advance.

Establish signs regarding when it is okay to steal a base and drill them into your players on a daily basis. Go over the signals after every practice and make sure your players know that they need to keep the signs to themselves and not share them with their friends on other teams.

Let your players know that you will be flashing the signs from the dugout or third base coaching box and that they need to pay attention to you prior to every pitch. This includes the hitter as well.

A Glance

- When attempting a stolen base, a quick glance back to determine whether the ball has been put into play is not a bad idea.

- Ideally, as a player gets older and gains more experience, he will be able to determine what is hap-

pening around him without glancing back.

- The runner can also get a better feel for watching the body language of whoever is covering second or third base on the attempted steal.

Commit

- The runner must be decisive. Once he has committed to run, he should run.

- The runner should continue his attempt at advancing to the next base. At the younger levels, most catchers cannot throw out a would-be base stealer with any great degree of

frequency, so the odds are in his favor.

- Stopping midway and returning to the original base is inadvisable. The runner will more often than not get caught in a rundown and be tagged out.

BASERUNNING

219

RUNNING FROM SECOND

Knowing when to run and when to stop is an important part of taking off from second base

When a runner is on second base, he has a great responsibility. He is in a position to score a run and make a difference in the game. Therefore he needs to be aware of everything that is going on around him.

The runner on second needs to pay attention to where the ball is hit. He needs to be aware of his third base coach and what signals he is giving. He needs to be cognizant of where the infielders are and whether they are attempting to sneak in behind him for a pickoff attempt. He needs to keep an eye on the pitcher and the catcher as well.

There is a great deal going on if you are a runner on second base, and the more prepared that runner is before he reaches

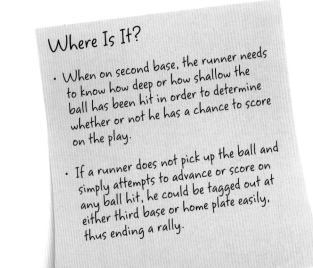

Where Is It?

- When on second base, the runner needs to know how deep or how shallow the ball has been hit in order to determine whether or not he has a chance to score on the play.

- If a runner does not pick up the ball and simply attempts to advance or score on any ball hit, he could be tagged out at either third base or home plate easily, thus ending a rally.

Third Base Coach

- Runners advancing from second base or around second base coming from first need to watch the third base coach. He is there for a reason.

- The third base coach is watching the play unfold and will help determine whether the runner has an opportunity to score.

- The runner should not ignore the third base coach when he puts up the stop sign. He is telling you to stay on third base for a reason.

second base, the better the results will be when he is asked to move off the base. Generally, the coach or manager will be the one in the third base coaching box, flashing signals on steals, bunts, and when to stop at third base or attempt to score on a base hit.

The runner on second base needs to pay attention to his coach. If he follows the coach's direction, then anything that goes wrong—being thrown out at the plate or on an attempted steal—will be on the coach and not on the player. That is the way it should be. If the runner chooses to run on his own or blow through the stop sign when the coach is giving it, then he alone is responsible when the results are disastrous.

Even if the results turn out to be positive, the player should be admonished. It is imperative that the players always listen to the coach under all circumstances when it comes to baseball. He is the coach and the one in charge for a reason.

Where Are They?

- When a runner is on second base, he needs to keep an eye on where the second baseman and shortstop are in relation to the base.

- A good infielder can be very stealthy and sneak up behind the runner at second base and apply a tag on a pickoff throw.

- Runners should be aware where the infielders are and not stray too far off the base unless the shortstop and second baseman are not in the vicinity.

Seize the Moment

- The runner on second base should seize the opportunity when there is a right-handed batter at the plate and less than two outs. This is the best time to attempt a steal of third base.

- A coach should discourage an attempted steal of third base when there are two outs. It is never good to make the third out at third base and waste a runner that had been in scoring position.

RUNNING FROM THIRD

A knowledgeable runner can do a great deal of damage to the opposition when on third base

A runner on third base can be more of an asset to the team at bat than the obvious. Sure, he's 90 feet away and can score on a shallow base hit or a sacrifice fly/grounder if there are less than two outs. He can also be the catalyst for a big inning if he pays attention and follows some safety guidelines when taking his lead.

Encourage your players to be pests once they have reached third base. Creating a distraction can ultimately ruffle a pitcher and lead not only to the runner on third scoring but also to his allowing several more runners to reach base. While creating a distraction is a good idea, remind your players that they have to do so within the guidelines of good sportsmanship.

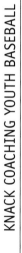

The Lead

- The runner should put his dancing shoes on and start doing a little bit of a tap up and down the line in an effort to distract the pitcher.

- The third baseman will rarely be holding the runner on because he is busy focusing on the batter. Therefore the runner has a bit more freedom with taking a lead than if he is on first or second.

- The runner should make that freedom count and be a distraction to the pitcher, breaking to the plate and then dancing back to the base.

Foul Territory

- While the runner can have some fun attempting to distract the pitcher, he should do so by standing in foul territory.

- If the runner is in fair territory and gets hit by a batted ball, then he is out, so he should always be cognizant of where he is standing.

- Standing in foul territory will also keep him out of the right-handed hitter's line of vision and prevent him from being a distraction in that regard.

Dancing off the base and faking a steal of home—that's fine. Taking a quick succession of leads and running back to the base in an aggressive manner—that's fine, too. What isn't acceptable is screaming, jumping, or taunting the pitcher. The runner needs to realize that he is in the position of power and can do a great deal to help his teammate at the plate by taking the pitcher's mind off his real task—focusing on the hitter.

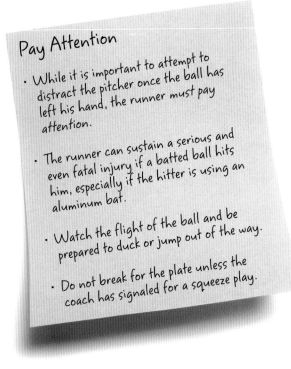

Pay Attention

- While it is important to attempt to distract the pitcher once the ball has left his hand, the runner must pay attention.

- The runner can sustain a serious and even fatal injury if a batted ball hits him, especially if the hitter is using an aluminum bat.

- Watch the flight of the ball and be prepared to duck or jump out of the way.

- Do not break for the plate unless the coach has signaled for a squeeze play.

Tagging Up

- A runner cannot officially leave any base on a fly ball until the fielder has caught the ball.

- The runner may stray off the base a few feet and prepare to run in the event the fielder drops the ball or does not catch it. If the fielder catches the ball, though, the runner must return to the base and tag up—touch the base—before advancing.

- If the runner fails to tag up, the fielder can simply throw the ball to the base that was vacated for a double play.

BASERUNNING

223

SLIDING
Drop but don't stop as you work your way into the sliding position

Sliding is one of the most difficult aspects of the game to teach and perfect for a variety of reasons. Let's start with the players themselves. Most youngsters do not have the coordination to slide properly. They flop and fall, stop and drop, and usually have a hard time with figuring out how to make their bodies twist and turn the proper way to slide.

That is okay. There are going to be growing pains—along with some bumps, bruises, and raspberries—associated with

teaching younger players how to slide. Be patient with them and enjoy the fun of watching them learn this very important skill.

An easy way to teach them how to slide is actually away from the field. Find someone who has a big enough backyard, get a slip and slide, hook it up to a hose, and let the kids go to work. Make a party out of it. This will help with team morale, provide some bonding time, and give them the

Feet First

- Regardless of what youngsters see on television, they should not try to slide headfirst into a base.

- The proper way to slide into a base is feet first.

- Headfirst slides can lead to injuries. Far too often, players jam fingers, either on the

base or the opposing player, hurt their hips or ribs, and are more susceptible to head and neck injuries.

- A feet-first slide will also afford the runner the opportunity to knock the ball out of the fielder's hand or prevent her from continuing the play.

First Base

- The runner should never, ever slide into first base.

- The runner will always get to first base quicker if he runs as hard as he can through the base. The time it takes to dip into the slide takes away precious seconds that invariably lead to the runner being called out.

- The runner should not dive headfirst into first base for the reasons mentioned in the previous section.

- It is okay for the runner to dive or duck under a tag on a wild throw that pulls the first baseman off the bag.

necessary prep time for when they actually have to slide in a game.

The one drawback to working on sliding regards the fields themselves. Many Little League fields around the country are not in pristine shape. The dirt can be hard or packed; it can be gravelly or worse. Trying to teach a player how to slide on such a field can be dangerous and painful. Make certain that when you are preparing to teach your players how to slide, you have sufficiently scouted out the field and have determined that it is safe to work on.

Explain to your players that sliding isn't easy and that they can develop raspberries on their thighs from sliding. A good pair of sliding shorts underneath the uniform pants will solve and or prevent that problem.

The Traditional Slide

- Sliding should be a continuation of running. Do not slow down as you fall into a slide; it will take away from the act of sliding itself and lead to possible injury.

- The runner must decide the side of the body which he will slide on. If he chooses the left side, it will be his left leg that he tucks up under his body as he leans to his left side with the slide and vice versa.

- The leg that is not tucked under will be extended toward the base.

The Hook Slide

- The hook slide is a variation of the traditional slide.

- As the runner dips into his slide, he is actually sliding away from the base to the side opposite the one on which the fielder has taken position.

- As the runner nears the base, he actually angles his body away from the base, bends his lead leg and grazes the corner of the base with his foot, hooking it.

- This slide presents a much smaller target for the fielder to tag.

HELPFUL HINTS

A few helpful tips can be a big factor in becoming a better ballplayer

The last section of this book is about common sense. As a coach, you have to have it. As a player, you hope that it will come with time if it isn't already there. That's why the tips discussed in this section are so useful. They are all based on common sense.

Coaches need to impress on their players the need to pay attention. It's a lesson that will help them not only in baseball but in life as well. Focus on the task at hand, whether it is running the bases or studying for a history exam. If you can get the youngsters in your care to focus and remain that way, you are halfway to becoming a successful coach.

Get them to hustle as well. No one likes a slacker, and if you

Look and Listen

- The base coaches are there for a reason. They are the runners' eyes and ears when they are steaming around the bases, deciding whether or not to try to score or grab an extra base.

- The runners need to listen to and watch their coaches at all times when on the bases. It is important for them to remember that the coaches have a better view of how the play has unfolded and are capable of making a more informed decision on whether to advance the extra base.

The On-deck Hitter

- Often overlooked, the on-deck hitter can play an important role during a rally.

- There is no coach at home plate to tell the runner what to do, so that responsibility falls on the on-deck hitter.

- He can move closer to the plate from the on-deck circle and instruct the incoming runner whether to slide or come in standing up.

- The signal for coming in standing up is to stand up straight with the arms stretched directly into the air. Patting the hands in the air, as if patting the ground, is the signal for a slide.

have players on your team that are giving less than 100 percent, their teammates will pick up on it. Explain to them the difficult situation it will put everyone in if there are one or two players on the squad who do not give their best effort at every juncture of the game.

You want everyone to have fun. Essentially that is what this is all about. Baseball is a game meant to be enjoyed. There shouldn't be division or stress on your team simply because some players do not wish to cooperate. Lay down the law early and be the coach you know you can be. Take charge,

be firm but gentle when it is needed, and remember that they are only kids. Treat them as such and cherish the time you spend with them. It is a special period in their lives and should be so in yours as well.

Be Aware

- We have discussed at great length throughout the book the importance of being aware. It bears repeating here.

- The runner should be aware of where the ball is at all times when you are on the basepaths. He should know where it was hit, who has it, and be able to determine how quickly the ball can be thrown across the diamond, back to the infield, etc.

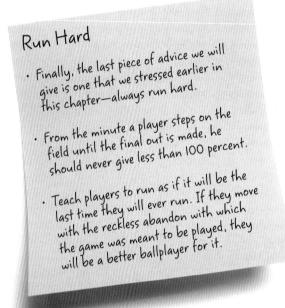

Run Hard

- Finally, the last piece of advice we will give is one that we stressed earlier in this chapter—always run hard.

- From the minute a player steps on the field until the final out is made, he should never give less than 100 percent.

- Teach players to run as if it will be the last time they will ever run. If they move with the reckless abandon with which the game was meant to be played, they will be a better ballplayer for it.

227

RESOURCES

Baseball has been played for nearly a century and a half. While some of the rules have changed through the years, the basic principles of the game have remained the same. The following list of resources will provide a good jumping off point for finding other information regarding coaching youth baseball. There are hundreds of books and Web sites dedicated to this subject so be sure and check the library, local bookstores, and the Internet for extra titles.

Books

American Sports Education Program, *The Rookie Coaches Baseball Guide,* Human Kinetics (1993)

James Buckley Jr., *The Visual Dictionary of Baseball,* Dorling Kindersl (2001)

Jeff Burroughs, *Jeff Burroughs' Little League Instructional Guide,* Bon Books (1994)

John McCarthy Jr., *Youth Baseball—The Guide for Coaches and Paren* Betterway Books (1996)

Ned McIntosh, *Managing Little League Baseball, A Little League Ba: ball Guide,* McGraw-Hill (1st ed., 1985)

Organizations

Babe Ruth Baseball
www.baberuthleague.org

PONY League Baseball
www.pony.org

Reviving Baseball In Inner Cities (RBI)
www.mlb.com/mlb/official_info/community/rbi.jsp

T-Ball USA Association
www.tballusa.org

World Baseball Association
www.wbabaseball.org

Periodicals

www.juniorbaseball.com

RESOURCES

Sporting Goods Companies

Akadema Pro
www.akademapro.com

Easton
www.eastonsports.com

Mizuno Sporting Goods
www.mizuno.com

Rawlings
www.rawlings.com

Wilson Sporting Goods
www.wilson.com

Web Sites

www.baseballbats.net

www.littleleague.org

www.oncoachingkidsbaseball.com

www.qcbaseball.com

www.thelittleleaguecoach.com

www.travelballselect.com

Web Sites for Fans

Baseball History
www.baseballreference.com

Major League Baseball
www.mlb.com

Minor League Baseball
www.milb.com

Youth Baseball for Children with Special Needs

www.littleleague.org/Learn_More/About_Our_Organization/divisions/challenger.htm

The Challenger Division was established in 1989 as a separate division of Little League Baseball. It provides boys and girls between the ages of five and eighteen who have physical and mental challenges the opportunity to play youth baseball in a friendly, accepting environment.

RESOURCES

CHECKLISTS

Even though all of this information is in the book, sometimes it's handy to have a checklist in front of you before you head to practice or a game. Here are a few checklists that you might find useful.

Player Gear

- ❑ balls
- ❑ bats
- ❑ batting gloves
- ❑ cleats
- ❑ eye black (for older kids)
- ❑ glove
- ❑ hat
- ❑ socks
- ❑ sun screen
- ❑ uniform
- ❑ water

Practice Checklist

- ❑ ball bag: an easy way to carry both the balls and the ext equipment
- ❑ bat bag: an easy way to carry as many as a dozen baseba bats
- ❑ cell phone: handy in an emergency
- ❑ bases: some fields don't have bases, so it's always a goc idea to keep some in your trunk
- ❑ emergency forms: these usually have contact informatio and medical information for each player
- ❑ first aid kit: should include bandages and ice packs, amon other items
- ❑ whistle: allows the coach to get the players' attention

Game Checklist

- ❏ balls: new, clean balls should be used in every game
- ❏ ball bag: extra balls are good for warm-up before game.
- ❏ cell phone: handy in an emergency
- ❏ clipboard: keeps papers—rosters, emergency forms, player cards, etc.—all in one place
- ❏ emergency forms: these usually have contact information and medical information for each player
- ❏ first-aid kit: should include bandages and ice packs, among other items
- ❏ pen or pencil: to make changes in rosters or lineups or make notations
- ❏ water: coaches should bring plenty of water to keep the kids hydrated

Tryouts Checklist

- ❏ ball bag full of balls
- ❏ cell phone: handy in an emergency
- ❏ list of players trying out
- ❏ pen or pencil for notes
- ❏ clipboard: a hard surface to write notes on
- ❏ emergency forms: these usually have contact information and medical information for each player
- ❏ first-aid kit: should include bandages and ice packs, among other items
- ❏ whistle: gets the attention of a large group

GLOSSARY

Around the Horn: Refers to a double play that is started by the third baseman, who throws the ball to the second baseman for a force play. The second baseman then throws to first to complete the double play.

Assist: A number that is credited to every player who touches a batted ball prior to a putout. For example, on a grounder to short in which the shortstop throws the runner out at first, he would be credited with an assist.

At-bat: A plate appearance that is officially credited to the batter. A player is not credited with an at-bat on a walk, a hit by pitch, a sacrifice fly, or if the inning ends while he is in the batters box and a runner is caught stealing or picked off.

Balk: An illegal motion made by a pitcher that will allow a runner to advance a base.

Bases on Balls: The official name for a walk.

Batter's Box: The chalked-off areas on either side of home plate in which the batter stands during an at-bat. They are 4 feet wide and 6 feet long and begin 6 inches away from the plate.

Battery: The pitcher and the catcher.

Batting Average: A statistic calculated by dividing a player's number of hits by his at-bats. For example, if a player has nine hits in twenty-seven at-bats, he is hitting .333.

Bunt: This occurs when a batter holds the bat loosely in his fingers and guides it into the ball, attempting to tap it lightly into fair territory.

Catcher: The player positioned behind home plate.

Changeup: An off-speed pitch that is not thrown as rapidly as a fastball. A circle change and straight changeup are just two examples.

Check Swing: This occurs when a batter begins to swing but holds up and does not complete his swing. An umpire will use his discretion to determine when a swing was checked or not.

Choke Up: The act of a batter moving his hands up on the bat in order to have better control of it while swinging.

Closer: The pitcher who attempts to "close" or finish the game for the winning team.

Count: The acting of keeping track of balls and strikes is the count. Balls are generally first when discussing a count. For example, if the count was two and one, there would be two balls and one strike.

Curveball: A breaking pitch with diagonal spin that causes tremendous movement.

Double Play: A double play occurs when two outs are recorded during one plate appearance.

Earned Run Average: A pitching statistic calculated by multiplying the number of earned runs a pitcher allows by nine and then dividing that number by his total number of innings pitched.

Error: A player is charged with an error when the official scorer deems him to have misplayed a ball hit to him or after he has made an errant throw.

First Baseman: The player traditionally positioned in fair territory near first base.

Fly Ball: Any ball that is hit high in the air.

Force Out: This occurs when a batter is "forced" to leave the basepath during another player's at-bat because he is thrown out while attempting to advance to a particular base.

Foul Ball: Any ball not hit in fair territory.

Full Count: When the batter has worked the count to three balls and two strikes, the count is full.

Ground Ball: Any ball hit on the ground.

Hit and Run: This occurs when the baserunners are in motion before the ball is hit. The runner then attempts to make contact in order to keep the runners moving.

Infield: The infield is composed of the four players who are positioned around the bases and in the basepaths. The first baseman, second baseman, third baseman, and shortstop are the infielders.

Intentional Walk: An intentional walk occurs when a pitcher and catcher elect to throw four balls purposely outside the strike zone in order not to face a particular batter.

Knuckleball: A breaking ball that is gripped with the knuckles rather than the fingertips. The pitch dances and changes trajectory as it approaches the plate.

Long Reliever: A pitcher that comes into a game early to replace the starter and pitches an extraordinarily long time, say five or six innings.

Middle Reliever: A pitcher who pitches an inning or two, usually the fifth, sixth, or sometimes seventh innings.

On Deck: The on-deck batter is the one who is up next in the batting order after the batter who is currently at the plate.

Outfield: The outfield is the area from foul line to foul line beyond the infield.

Outfielder: A player who is positioned in the area from foul line foul line beyond the infield. The outfielders are the left fielder, rig fielder, and center fielder.

Pinch Hitter: A pinch hitter is a substitute batter for the regula scheduled batter.

Pinch Runner: A pinch runner is a substitute runner for any runn who has reached base safely.

Pop Fly: Any batted ball that is hit in the air.

Run Batted In: Also known as an RBI, the run batted in is a statist credited to a hitter when his plate appearance results in a run bein scored. No RBI is credited in certain instances, such as when the ba ter has reached base on an error.

Runners at the Corners: Refers to when there are runners on fir and third base.

Sacrifice Fly: Not an official at-bat under baseball scoring rule though it is a productive one. It occurs when a ball is hit in the air in the outfield with less than two outs and the runner on base advance or scores.

Save: A pitcher is credited with a save when he finishes the gam for the winning team though he is not the winning pitcher. A save recorded if the pitcher pitches at least a third of an inning and ente a game with a lead of no more than three runs. A save is also credite when a pitcher pitches at least three innings or if the potential tyin or winning run is on deck, at bat, or on base.

Scoring Position: Any runner on second or third base is in scorin position.

Second Baseman: The player positioned between first and second base.

Setup Man: The pitcher who usually pitches the seventh and/or eighth inning, thus setting up the opposing lineup for the closer, who pitches the ninth inning.

Shortstop: The player positioned between second and third base.

Slider: A pitch that starts out looking like a fastball but breaks sharply as it nears the plate, either into or away from the hitter.

Squeeze: A squeeze play is a sacrifice bunt with less than two outs and a runner on third base.

Steal: A stolen base occurs when a runner successfully moves up a base while the pitcher is delivering a pitch.

Strike: Any pitch that is determined by the umpire to be over the plate when a batter has not swung. A batter can also swing and miss a pitch for a strike. A foul ball is also a strike, but a batter cannot strike out on a foul ball unless it is bunted.

Strike Zone: The area above home plate that stretches from the batter's armpits to his knees, measuring the width of the plate.

Switch Hitter: A player who can hit from both the right and left-hand sides of the plate.

Third Baseman: The player who plays on the left side of the infield at third base.

Walk: Also known as a base on balls, a walk occurs when a pitcher throws four balls to one batter in a single at-bat.

INDEX

241